Cold War or Détente in the 1980s

Cold War or Détente in the 1980s

The International Politics of American–Soviet Relations

Peter Savigear

St. Martin's Press
New York

First published in the United States of America in 1987

Printed in Great Britain

ISBN 0-312-00437-0

Library of Congress Cataloging-in-Publication Data

Savigear, Peter.
  Cold War or Détente in the 1980s.

  Bibliography: p.
  Includes index.
   1. United States — Foreign relations — Soviet Union.
  2. Soviet Union — Foreign relations — United States.
  3. United States — Foreign relations — 1981 —
  4. Soviet Union — Foreign relations — 1975 —
  I. Title.
  E183.8.S65S275 1987   327.73047   86-26254
  ISBN 0-312-00437-0

Contents

Preface

The author of this essay in international relations owes a great debt to many people for their willingness to discuss the events and themes which are the substance of the work. The interest, advice and critical comment of friends, colleagues and acquaintances were all invaluable. In some cases very particular information was made available. These many people have contributed something; too numerous to list and to risk any omission, they all have my thanks. The interpretation and arguments are all my responsibility. Two other acknowledgements are in order: Leicester University provided some financial help; my wife, Francine, and Mandy, Richard and Juliet, provided patience beyond measure for allowing the typing to ruin holidays and dominate family life.

Key Dates and Events in the 1980s

1979

7 January	Kampuchea. Vietnamese forces assisted in capture of Phnom-Penh.
26 March	Egypt/Israel agreement at Camp David, USA.
4 November	Iran. 98 hostages held in US embassy, Teheran.
12 December	NATO ministers agreed on intermediate range missile deployment, the 'Twin-track' decison.
26 December	Afghanistan. Soviet troops invaded.

1980

24 March	El Salvador. Assassination of Archbishop Romero.
7 April	USA broke diplomatic relations with Iran.
17 April	People's Republic of China joined International Monetary Fund.
24 April	Iran. US attempt to rescue hostages failed.
19 May	Warsaw meeting between Mr Brezhnev and President Giscard d'Estaing.
22 June	Venice Declaration on Palestine, an agreed European Community policy.
19 July	Moscow Olympic Games opened.
4 September	Iraq invaded Iran.
9 September	Madrid opening of Conference on Security and Cooperation in Europe.
4 December	El Salvador. Bodies of four American nuns found, after their assassination.

1981

1 January	European Community Lomé Convention II came into operation.
20 January	US hostages from the embassy siege leave Iran.
10 May	Election of socialist President Mitterrand in France.
19 August	Gulf of Sirte. Dog fight between US and Libyan aircraft.
6 October	President Sadat assassinated.
22 October	Cancun, Mexico, conference on North/South economic cooperation.
18 November	'Zero-zero' solution proposed by President Reagan.

1982

1 January	Spain joined NATO.
1 January	Appointment of Perez de Cuellar as UN Secretary General.
2 April	Argentinian invasion of the Falkland Islands.
April	Sinai. Final stage of agreed Israeli withdrawal.
6 June	Lebanon invasion by Israeli forces.
14 June	Argentinian surrender to UK forces in Falklands.
22 June	Chad government formed by Hissene Habre.

1983

23 March	Strategic Defence Initiative announced.
3 May	USSR agreed to include warheads, not just missiles in arms negotiations.
13 August	Chad. French Operation Manta began, against Libyan supported rebels in the North.
27 August	Soviet offer on missiles and warheads, to include British and French nuclear forces.
10 July	Poland. Martial law ended.
31 August	South Korean airliner shot down by Soviet fighters.
9 September	Republic of South Africa revised constitution approved, creating chambers for Indians and Coloureds.
26 September	US revised position on arms control announced.
23 October	US and French forces attacked in Beirut with many casualties.
25 October	Grenada invaded by US troops after assassination of Prime Minister Maurice Bishop.

17 November	French air attack on sites near Baalbek.
31 December	Formal operational deployment of cruise missiles, Greenham Common, UK, followed by deployment in Federal Germany and Italy.

1984

1 January	USSR delivered first natural gas consignment through Siberian pipeline to France.
14 January	Athens. Balkan states discussed nuclear free zone for the region.
17 January	Stockholm Conference on confidence-building measures opened.
16 March	Vienna talks resumed on balanced force reduction.
16 March	Nkomati agreement between Republic of South Africa and Mozambique signed, on terrorist activity and non-aggression.
16 March	US troops finally left four power Beirut peace-keeping force.
10 May	International Court forbade US mining of Nicaraguan ports.
14 May	USSR deployed new missiles in East Germany.
14 June	Dutch parliament postponed decision on deployment of cruise missiles in Netherlands.
25 July	East and West Germany agreed on easier trading conditions.
28 July	Los Angeles Olympic Games opened.
4 September	Herr Honecker of East Germany postponed visit to the Federal Republic.
9 September	Bulgarian leader Todov Zhivkov cancelled planned visit to Federal Germany.
26 September	Hong Kong agreement between UK and Chinese People's Republic.
27 October	'Rome Declaration' by the member states of the West European Union on the future of the organisation.
30 October	Body of Father Popieluszko, supporter of Polish union Solidarity, found after his murder.
31 October	Assassination of Mrs Gandhi in India.
22 November	USA and USSR announced new round of arms control talks for 1985.
18 December	Mr Gorbachev visited UK.

1985

7 January	Geneva arms control talks initiated by Mr Gromyko and Mr Schultz.
24 March	US Major Arthur Nicholson shot while serving on the military liaison commission in East Germany.
7 April	USSR announced a freeze in the deployment of medium range missiles.
1 May	USA applied economic sanctions to Nicaragua.
2 July	Mr Gromyko retired as Soviet foreign minister, to become President of USSR.
10 July	Greenpeace ship *Rainbow Warrior* sunk by French agents in Auckland, New Zealand.
25 November	Geneva summit talks between President Reagan and Mr Gorbachev.

1986

1 January	Spain and Portugal became members of the European Community.
14 April	US air raid on Libyan cities.
26 April	Chernobyl nuclear disaster.

CHANGES OF GOVERNMENT AND ELECTORAL RESULTS OF INTERNATIONAL SIGNIFICANCE

1980

5 October	West Germany. Social democratic/Free democratic coalition success in legislative elections.
4 November	USA presidential elections. Ronald Reagan elected.

1981

26 April/10 May	France. Presidential elections. M Mitterrand elected on second ballot.
14/21 June	Socialist success in French legislative elections.

1982

26 September	Amin Gemayel replaced the assassinated president of Lebanon, Bashir Gemayel.
28 October	Spain. Socialist success in legislative elections.

1983

6 March	West German legislative elections. Christian democratic/Free democratic elections.
9 June	UK general elections. Conservative success.
16 June	USSR. Yury Andropov elected President of the Presidium of Supreme Soviet after death of Leonid Brezhnev.
4 August	Italian coalition government led by Sig Craxi.
8 August	Guatemala *coup d'etat* led by General Victores.
15 September	Mr Begin resigned in Israel.
10 December	Argentinian democratic government led by Sen Alfonsin.

1984

13 February	USSR. Mr Chernenko became General Secretary of Soviet Communist Party after the death of Yury Andropov.
4 November	Nicaragua general election. Sandinistas re-elected.
6 November	USA presidential election. Mr Reagan re-elected.

1985

15 January	Brazil returned to civilian rule. President elect, Dr Neves.
11 March	Mikhail Gorbachev elected General Secretary of Soviet Communist Party after death of Mr Chernenko.
6 April	Sudan. President Numeiry deposed.
28 July	Peru. Inauguration of President Alan Garcia, bringing the success of the *Alianza Popular Revolucconaria Americana*.

1986

16 March	France. M Chirac heads a centre-right coalition after legislative elections.

Introduction: New Perspectives

The United States and the Soviet Union loom over all aspects of international relations, still reducing other factors to a miserable impotence. This is how it seems at the beginning of the last two decades of the twentieth century. The dominant feature of the world is the same as it has been for several years—the primacy of the two superpowers. But there are also trends at work in the 1980s which threaten to undermine this dominance. Some are economic, others political and military. They are not all new or recent, but the coincidence of such trends seems different.

The following chapters assess the fate of the United States and the Soviet Union in the face of predominant trends in international relations. They are not a chronological account of the years 1980–86, but an attempt to show how the superpowers have been affected by the events and developments of these years. Whilst the period seems above all to lack a definite direction or logic, coherence and order were discernable and capable of analysis. One question which constantly recurs is whether the term 'superpower' retains any meaning as a result of the changes that have taken place in international relations.

Not least among the developments of the years 1980–86 was a confusion over the principles according to which the two greatest states organised their policies. What relevance had they? Some argued that conflict between the two states had pushed the clash of principles between capitalism and communism into the background by the 1980s. The correlation between the policies of the United States and the Soviet Union and their political principles was not immediately apparent. In 1985, when Mr Gorbachev succeeded Mr Chernenko as the youngest Soviet leader since Joseph Stalin, and brought to his appointment vigour, an easy personal charm and an attractive wife, the conflict became something like a duel between this very different Russian leader and the President of the United States, Ronald Reagan, who had been elected for a second term of office the same year. The relevance of ideology and the principles behind foreign policy seemed ever more remote. The two so-called superpowers were regarded with a mixture of frightened disillusion and of hope, because they still determined the stability of most of the world—at least their governments controlled more weapons and had more political influence than any other governments.

The application of principles to foreign policies seems more remote because both the USA and the USSR are widely presented as imperial states. Despite the widespread condemnation of the involvement of the United States in Vietnam, including that of the closest allies in Europe and the self-criticism which followed that war, a bleak conclusion was drawn: only lessons of secondary importance could be learned; political intervention and even belligerent involvement were perhaps inescapable from such great powers. Since 1973, and particularly since 1980, both have remained embroiled—the United States in the Middle East, Africa and Latin America, the Soviet Union in Eastern Europe, Africa and the Middle East. The military operation by the Soviet Union in Afghanistan, starting in December 1979, was a dramatic demonstration of superpower iniquity. The two states are trapped in a competition from which there seems to be no escape. There is little scope for freedom of choice. The principles and aims are those imposed by their rivalry. In that sense the two states are comparable, and the demands of their competition still seem endless in the 1980s; or so it seems. But the superpowers have made choices. Without choice of policy, there could be no errors, no evil, no judgement or condemnation.

The conditions in which the United States and the Soviet Union operate are significantly different, and the application of their principles and ideology are also special. The struggle for power and advantage has not totally obscured the political principles, although the ways in which ideology and intention direct and create policy are not obvious. The overriding characteristic of the superpowers was their common responsibility for power and principle in international relations. Principles and ideologies continued to affect the fundamentally different policies of the Soviet Union and the United States and of their allies. But in the conflicts of international politics the relevance was often hidden in the confusion.

The vocabulary in the discussion of international relations acquired some new names in the 1980s. The interested public learned of the existence of the Strait of Hormuz, the Gulf of Sirte, Managua, Basra and Haag Island, Port Stanley and Goose Green, Kaboul and the Bekaa Valley. The more knowledgeable knew of Asmara and N'Djamena. These and other places indicated new foci of tension and conflict. They reflected different preoccupations, but begged the question whether anything really significant had changed in the years from 1979 to 1985/1986.

There were few victors in the 1980s. The British secured a military surrender in the Falkland Islands in 1982; governments collapsed and new regimes appeared; but there were few heroes and few outright victors. The new names did not readily reveal any special quality which characterised international relations in the 1980s. There were no new international political organisations which submitted the governments of states to their authority. Indeed, by 1986, there were fears that the government of the United States might substantially cut its contribution to the United Nations Organisation. That contribution amounted to some 25 per cent of the total funds. The USA had already withdrawn from the United Nations Educational, Scientific and Cultural Organisation in 1984, essentially because it was believed to be pro-communist and wasteful of resources. Despite the new names, there seemed few fundamental changes in international politics and the dominant position of the United States and the Soviet Union. The world revealed a respect for traditional roles and institutions.

The heroes of international relations, and therefore of this book, remain states, not governments and politicians, especially not politicians. The heroes were the political communities themselves. They survived the dominance of the 'super-states' and supranational institutions. Peoples without states continued to seek the creation of stable states in the 1980s. Economic pressures implied the erosion of the state as the essential political institution in international relations, but these also failed. Currencies and economies withstood the demands for the greater interdependence of states and therefore the erosion of their economic autonomy. International corporations and trading companies continued to operate on terms ultimately decided by sovereign states. Thus developments in the world of states were not dramatically different in their mode of operation as the twentieth century entered its last two decades. Many of the features of international relations in the 1980s would have been familiar in earlier years. War and peace, the erosion of sovereignty, the presence of transnational 'actors' (perhaps the word acquired a new meaning after 1981) and their limitations, demands for independence and regional political autonomy, had all a history in international politics. Among the familiar features, however, the resilience of the state was foremost.

Although many of the conflicts of the interstate world were much the same, it was not always clear what had importance and what had proved ephemeral. The traditional post-war role of the superpowers was being eroded and this erosion became ever clearer. A serious contradiction occurred between the political leadership of the USA and the USSR and their overwhelming military strength, their economic resources and technical skills. There was no longer a universal conviction that even the economies and technical brilliance of the superpowers were unchallenged. In the 1980s there were regular predictions of Soviet economic collapse, and openly expressed fears about the fate of the American dollar. Dramatic and tragic disasters like the explosion at the Soviet nuclear power station at Chernobyl and the series of failures in the United States rocket, space and missile programmes, culminating in the loss of the Challenger space-craft with the loss of seven lives, demonstrated the limits of superpower skills to the world. Yet more blatant was the change in their political roles.

The USA and USSR became less important in international politics in the 1980s. Their role as superpowers was still significant, but economic and political developments in the world of states, had undermined the once almighty position of superpower. No state could challenge Soviet or American overall military capability, but these arsenals had less and less relevance to the day-to-day diplomatic and military intercourse. As the twentieth century entered the last two decades, the relationship between the superpowers, despite all the rhetoric and arms negotiations, was not the distinctive feature of international politics.

The argument of the following chapters concerns the relative importance of different levels and features of international relations: the military, the economic and the ideological. It is an attempt to assess the nature of relations between states, and especially those between the two superpowers as they face new challenges to their ideologies and their power, despite the continuing and remarkable weakness of truly international institutions. The survival of the state had been in great measure due to the success of the United States and the Soviet Union. Their integrity has withstood the challenge of political and economic interdependence, and they dominated any analysis of international relations in the 1980s. Yet the context in which they operate has changed. The connection between the interests of the superpowers and their ideologies is different. This is a recurrent theme in this essay in international relations. The assertion that is tested is that the significance of freedom to the foreign policy of the USA became greater than at any time since the years immediately following the Second World War.

The height of the Cold War was essentially a period of conflict between two ideologies. There was minimal political contact between the superpowers. The 1920s and the 1930s had barely seen the emergence of the Soviet Union into the world of states. Similarly the United States had hardly ventured into the Machiavellian world where ideology has little place and stable rule and the reconciliation of interests dominated—that is, the world of European international relations. Cold War was a reflection of isolated and ideological politics; relations between communism and the 'free world' were necessarily minimal. The basis of the 'détente' that followed the Cold War was the assumption that political interests were more important than ideology. The need for pragmatic agreements, and then for trade and social contacts, pushed ideological differences aside. *Ostpolitik,* Dr Kissinger's politics of 'linkage', and all the many political arrangements between ideologically opposed states, were the result of a different vision of international politics. The complicated drift through stages of Cold War and détente was never easy to chart. The movement was not direct and were often contradictory. Few would be arrogant enough to date definitive shifts from Cold War to détente. Like the dialectic of a fox-trot, a step backwards or sideways proved to be a step forwards. One feature was consistent—ideology declined in importance as a factor in relations between the United States and the USSR. This essay explores the proposition that this is no longer true in the 1980s.

A renewed preoccupation with ideology has been both part of the description of international politics since the late 1970s and a prescription for superpower relations. Ideology has thus been set against state interest and compromise in international relations, and has assumed a greater importance than some of the other trends, such as the declining international significance of Europe and the growth of economic interdependence.

The preoccupation of governments with an ideological foreign policy was essentially beyond challenge. There was an exclusivity about the assumptions behind any ideology. But this was also a relative matter. Ideology stood in opposition to a long tradition of compromise in international politics. This tradition was the distinctive feature of European international relations. All European governments learned to live within this tradition of compromise. Their ideologies had been trimmed to suit the prevailing currents of international diplomacy and this had often brought together states with conflicting beliefs about their internal ordering and about the evolution of international relations. Republican France and Imperial Russia were among the first and firmest of such allies in the twentieth century; Soviet Russia and Nazi Germany were among the more grotesque to seek a balance of power at the expense of ideological purity. This great tradition has not been lost on the present generation of European politicians, not least on those who live in the two Germanies of the late twentieth century. The degree of weight carried by ideology made a compromise more or less likely. Thus in Europe after 1945, the determination to pursue political considerations and negotiated settlements could not at first easily overcome the differences of principle between East and West. But it was overcome by the process known as détente. However the determination to apply ideology to international politics did not vanish with that process, and much of what occurred between 1980 and 1986 has a strongly ideological appearance.

Ideology and the practice of regular diplomacy were different in principle. The exclusivity of ideology ran counter to the need for political reconciliation of disputes. Thus ideological competition was essentially irreconcilable and the pursuit of a 'holy' war not amenable to negotiated settlement. The consideration of the role played by ideologies in international relations remained relevant to the 1980s. The European tradition had not excluded all political principles from the settlement of disputes. However the unassailable nature of some ideological arguments which allowed no compromise, implied a degree of interference in the internal affairs of other states. The demands of ideology cut across any political agreement which might imply the recognition of fundamental differences of principle. This was notably the case in southern Africa and in the Near and Middle East. The rejection of the policy of apartheid, adopted by the government of the Republic of South Africa, and the sweeping authoritarian claims of Islamic movements made truly political relations difficult to commence and sustain. The complete abandonment of the policy was demanded in the first case, and total political victory was required by the Iranian regime in the war with Iraq. Islamic ideology was essentially internationalist and fatalistic. For these reasons no meeting-point was possible between this belief and that which saw the need for compromise: hence the condemnation of the political settlement between the governments of Egypt and Israel achieved at the Camp David talks in 1979, orchestrated by the American President, Jimmy Carter. In 1983, 1984 and 1985, Pan-Arab conferences looked askance at the political reconciliation. In such ways the role of ideology distorted the politics of interest.

For many decades the USA had also injected an ideological passion into international relations. During the Second World War the push for total victory had been one such manifestation. Only slowly had government politicised the drive for freedom and modified the demand for total victory. The task had to be done again and again, in Korea and in Vietnam. A question for the 1980s was still how far ideology had returned to motivate the foreign policy of the United States at the expense of the diplomatic ingenuity achieved by Dr Henry Kissinger during his White House years. But the ideology of freedom at least suggested flexibility and debate, not fatalism and the exclusion of all alternative points of view. The analysis of the place of ideology in the policies of the United States remains crucial because of the continuing dominance of the United States in international politics. Despite the wishes of other governments, especially that of the Soviet Union, the USA was the colossus of international relations in 1980 as it had been in 1945. The following chapters, therefore, examine the position of the United States and the significance of this power for other states.

Not only has the fact of the superiority of the United States been contested, but it has also been obscured. Other questions about the nature of international relations in the 1980s have been given great emphasis. Has there been a second Cold War? How has such a Cold War passed, like that earlier one, without open hostilities between the Soviet Union and the USA? Have the 'superpowers' lost their significance?

In the years 1980–85 a flurry of publicly voiced fears clouded judgement of these questions. Hasty and partial assessments were invited from all manner of individuals and groups on the difficult questions of foreign and defence policy because they had become a public and controversial matter. The public debate was fired by the decisions of the governments of the United States and the Soviet Union to develop and finally to deploy new types of nuclear weapons. The procedures by which these weapons were prepared for deployment was not abrupt but drawn-out and extended over several years. This also encouraged public interest. The issue of the stationing of American-controlled cruise missiles in Western Europe, first raised by a decision in 1979 was still before the people of the Netherlands in 1986. An ill-informed and mostly speculative discussion commenced in 1983 on the possibilities of stationing defensive and offensive weapons in space. Thus the attention of all manner of people was focused on the superpowers and their relations in the 1980s.

Moreover since 1980 war has remained a constant element in international relations. More than a dozen substantial conflicts, involving more than one government, have erupted across the globe, from Latin America to the Near and Middle East, from the Sahara to southern Africa. The withdrawal of the last US troops from South Vietnam more than a decade ago did not bring peace to the people of South East Asia. The promise of a safer world which followed the improved relations between the USA and the USSR in the 1970s proved to be an illusion. While these two states groped towards a new understanding in 1975–85, a radical transformation came to the landscape of international relations. Familiar landmarks vanished. But at the same time a passionate concern with the prospect of nuclear war drew attention away from the deeper impact of these changes. Therefore the seemingly familiar aspect of the world of states in the 1980s reveals significant changes. The familiar has been challenged and a major upheaval threatened. The progress of détente in the 1980s has been uneven and ambiguous. Relations between the two superpowers and among their allies have been fundamentally altered. As the decade progresses, many of the stabilising elements in international politics have disappeared. Détente is not an adequate description of these less settled relations. Governments need to assess their policies again in the light of these events. Earlier judgements of policies have been undermined by the changed circumstances. Approval and condemnation are still necessary, but these judgements need revision.

The most basic change is in the understanding of which states are friendly and which hostile. Where this had been defined with a measure of certainty in 1970 or even in 1975, no such certainty exists in the 1980s. An accepted grasp of the good and the bad in international politics is missing. Moreover the growing obsession with nuclear arms makes such vital moral judgements more difficult. The search for a nuclear peace obscures other considerations. The preoccupation with weapons which affects Europe and North America and remote parts of the Pacific Ocean where fear of war and hostility to nuclear testing brought about changes of policy towards nuclear states, gave a special character to international relations. Concern with weapons and the balance of arms has implications for the place of ideology in the 1980s. Thus the peculiar quality of these years is not easy to define. Whereas earlier periods had been marked by firm and unequivocal turning-points, by events of generally agreed importance, the 1980s lack any such clear-cut signposts as the Truman Doctrine, the Berlin blockade, the Cuban missiles crisis or the Nixon initiatives of 1971–2. Through such pointers the world learned to recognise Cold War and détente. In contrast the slide from the heights of détente was less distinct. Superpower relations lost their coherence.

The relevance of freedom to international relations in particular was not as apparent in 1985 as it was in 1945. Yet that principle had been at the centre of the Cold War. The definition and application of freedom as an organising principle in international relations was the substance of the East–West tension that emerged from the peace of 1945. As the tension receded and the years of détente followed those of Cold War, freedom ceased to be the most important issue between the United States and the Soviet Union. The preoccupations of international politics had changed. Arguments about balance and power, particularly military power, came to dominate diplomacy between the great states of the contemporary world. These arguments were often posed in the language of political science. A kind of corruption had taken place. Political analysis of superpower relations had become divorced from the need to create freedom. The task of establishing institutions which increased the scope of human choice, the ideal in the name of which many had fought in the Second World War, had faded before the task of creating a military balance.

If the concern with freedom declined during the periods of détente, it did not easily return when tensions between East and

West began to sharpen later in the 1970s. The military balance continued to occupy centre stage. Freedom came to mean freedom from nuclear war. Freedom from war became more important in international relations than freedom to choose political institutions and priorities in the ordering of individual lives. The very nature of international relations has undergone a change and the 1980s seem to have a new quality, which is no longer a simple reflection of the qualities of Cold War or détente. In the face of these colossal questions about the nature of international relations, detailed changes occurred. The central role of Europe had shifted. The European states had long pulled back from major involvement outside the continent—with a few curious exceptions. Britain engaged in a war in the South Atlantic in 1982, and France was drawn into military entanglement in central Africa. Cold War began in Europe—not to say in Germany—but by 1980 European politics had ceased to be at the centre of international politics. Yet in the 1980s, Europe remains at the heart of the military relationship between the United States and the Soviet Union. Perhaps only in Europe is the status of a 'superpower' of any real significance as a result of the reality of the arms balance.

If Europe was preoccupied with military balance, other newer concerns complicated the underlying relations between East and West. What did the ideologies of the superpowers mean in the face of a new internationalism? National frontiers were breached by fresh movements. A compassionate concern with the environment and the hungry burst the constraints imposed by governments. Narrow national preoccupations were rejected by the strong common concern for the preservation of the planet. In Europe and North America, ecological protest found votes in the 1980s, although the votes and the success of ecology parties were not evenly spread; the Green Party in the Federal Republic of Germany was the most successful. This movement gained seats both at local (*Land* or provincial) level and at national level in the parliament or *Bundestag*. From 1.5 per cent of the vote in the national elections in 1980, their share rose to 5.6 per cent in 1983, earning the party 27 seats. Although the movements whose priorities were the environment, the concern for nature and the preservation of species were less politically successful elsewhere, they did exist and their aims did not stop at national frontiers. The organisation of market forces or the creation of a single party democracy were not their principal concerns. Because their priorities cross frontiers and state boundaries in a new way, they constitute an important fact for established governments and for the predominant ideologies of the United States and the Soviet Union.

State boundaries also appeared irrelevant to those movements which demanded action in support of the starving. The worst examples of contemporary famine seem to be in central Africa, particularly in the Sudan, Somalia and Ethiopia. Prolonged drought, in some areas of more than ten years' duration, made this tragedy conspicuous in the 1980s. The existing regimes had no monopoly of aid and they faced movements which grew in intensity and momentum. Some were very successful, like that of Band Aid; this movement earned millions of dollars in famine relief for Ethiopia and other causes.

The apparent irrelevance of the old East–West division was also shown by the distinction between rich and poor states, between North and South. A formal dialogue existed between the more prosperous states and the poorer, less industrially and commercially developed states. The capitalist and communist conflict, the tension between the two nuclear superpowers, was blurred by this distinction. It seemed that the older East–West divide was callous and indifferent to the plight of the needy. The fixed place of that ideological conflict disappeared. The international relevance of the two superpowers was threatened in a new way because the more important issues in the eyes of many people are secondary to the number of nuclear missiles which each possess or the principles according to which their politics and economics are organised.

The disappearance of the former East–West priorities permitted other shifts in international politics. Closer relations across political divides were possible. The atmosphere of politics changed, or at least became less certain. Such shifting moods were especially marked in superpower relations. Fluctuations in relations are replacing the much slower changes which characterised earlier periods. Hostility and harmony alternate rapidly in the 1980s. Within two years of the first deployment of cruise missiles in Europe, President Reagan was shaking the hand of Mr Gorbachev, the General Secretary of the Soviet Communist party. The Soviet delegation had left the bilateral arms talks with the United States after the cruise and Pershing 2 missiles were deployed in three West European states (the Federal Republic of Germany, Italy and the United Kingdom) in December 1983. Yet almost within months, the Soviet leader was urging improved relations. The American President proclaimed his determination to do better than his predecessors in sustaining improved relations with the Soviet Union. The Geneva meeting of November 1985 became a vital moment for the USA and the Soviet Union. Journalists wrote of the 'Geneva spirit'. The harmony was not blurred by the many spy scandals that took place during the years 1979–85, affecting not only the superpowers but other states, including the United Kingdom, France and West Germany. Other moments of tension were forgotten. There had been precedents. The Soviet leader had been well received in London by the British Prime Minister, Mrs Margaret Thatcher, in 1984, and she was both politically and personally close to the President of the United States. The antagonism that prevented the United States from competing in the Moscow Olympic Games of 1980 when Mr Carter was President, and the USSR from attending those at Los Angeles in 1984, was deliberately forgotten in the days of November 1985. On the occasion of the Geneva meeting, even the wives of the two leaders presented a vision of 'good neighbourliness'. Their much publicised talks and tea drinking provided the more than 2000 journalists who had gathered in Geneva with something to report, perhaps a poor recompense for the official 'blackout' of news from the political discussion.

Superpower relations with other governments were no more stable and coherent than their mutual contacts in the 1980s. In particular, the demonology of European states was confusing. Friendly overtures went hand in hand with denunciations. Poland lost its 'most favoured nation' status in trading relations with the USA. Other demonstrations of political disapproval had to live with the need for trade. Expanding East–West trade and developing economic relations were not lightly abandoned, and there was a degree of friction between governments whose economic interests did not coincide. At the lowest points of Soviet–American contact, in 1981 and especially in 1983–84 when the new intermediate-range missiles arrived in Western Europe, efforts were made by the Soviet Union to keep open channels to the government in Bonn. Despite the tension on defence matters, the Soviet Union was concerned to show the Federal Republic that the basis of economic relations between the two states was still 'sympatisch' and accommodating. Friendly contacts remained vigorous between these closest of European partners in the flourishing trade between East and West. Mr Gromyko, then still the Soviet Foreign Minister, reassured the government in Bonn. The curtailment of the plans for a visit by Mr Honecker, the East German political leader, to the Federal Republic was not permitted to intervene in the economic traffic between East and West. Such events occurred at the height of the drama concerning the deployment of missiles.

The upheavals which took place in the government of states gave a special thrust to international politics in the 1980s. Stable allies vanished and the isolation of the superpowers was more likely. Familiar governments disappeared, and their replacements required cautious revision of policy by the United States and the Soviet Union. Even in once secure regions, elections and *coups d'état* upset the established order of the 1960s and 1970s, and the government of the United States had to adjust to these developments. The appeal of communism and dependence on the USSR were no longer clear, and this correspondingly complicated the policies of the Soviets.

In Latin America the Sandinista government replaced the dictatorship in Nicaragua in 1979 and brought a Marxist regime to Central America. Other Cuban and Soviet influences were active in the region as well as the Caribbean. The fragility of established governments was regularly revealed. Military oligarchies gave way to democratic, civilian rule in Brazil and the Argentine—the latter after the war with the British. In 1985 the Peruvians had a Social Democratic government; the APRA party came to office for the first time. Elsewhere the USA also lost obvious allies of the past. In South-East Asia, the United States continued to support the government of Thailand. In

1986 the Marcos presidency collapsed after elections in the Philippines, and was replaced by that of Mrs Aquino, widow of a former rival of Mr Marcos.

The Soviet Union continued to support the state of Vietnam, but Russian allies were not secure. The Vietnamese thrust further into Cambodia, now known as Kampuchea. In 1979 the Soviet Union invaded Afghanistan. This event was received with public surprise by the United States and by West European governments. They condemned the invasion, but could not publically admit prior knowledge of the operation because that would have required some more definite action than the expression of disapproval. In these examples, previously accepted stable regimes and international loyalties were overturned or threatened.

The wars on the African continent were without direct or constant involvement from the Soviet Union and the United States. Some of the wars were not new. In Eritrea a long struggle for independence continued against the Marxist government of Ethiopia. In the Sudan, Mali and the western Sahara, insurgents and government forces fought shifting campaigns; and in Chad a war which also involved Libyan claims to the strip of territory on the northern border, the 'Band of Aozou', some 700 miles long and about 100 miles across, has been waged since the state gained its independence from France in 1960. These conflicts made the balance of power on the continent as uncertain in 1985 as it had been in 1975. These uncertainties in government mean that the precise political complexion of whole regions is unclear in the 1980s. It is much the same in southern Africa. Insurgents are still active in Angola, Mozambique, Namibia and to a lesser extent in Uganda and Zimbabwe. The suspicion that the Soviet Union has achieved a substantial political influence on the continent is not at all certain. Cuban troops remain in Angola. South African units are engaged on the frontiers of the Republic. Other local wars have occurred in the northern parts of the continent, and no positive alignment has emerged. Again the impression is one of new instability.

This generalisation is above all true of the Middle East. The results of the collapse of the Pahlavi regime in Iran were felt throughout the world. The United States lost a secure ally and an alliance. The Central Treaty Organisation, developed across the Near and Middle East since 1959, vanished with the Shah. No proper diplomatic relationship has been possible between the USA and Iran since then. And there has been little comfort for the Soviet Union either. The new regime is not sympathetic and the role of the Communist Party, the *Tudeh,* is indecisive, if always present. The war between Iran and Iraq, destructive, localised and murderous, disrupted political relations in the entire Gulf area from 1980 to 1986. Military balances, oil prices and production, economic prospects were all thrown into the air by this war, a direct result of the change of government in Iran and the swing towards Shiite Islamic ideology.

The damaging effects of the war in the Persian Gulf coincided with the isolation of Egypt. The leading role that had been taken by the government in Cairo since the revolutionary change of 1952 was lost. Egypt was isolated from its Arab neighbours in politics if not in economic or physical reality following the Camp David agreement, although by 1985 there were other political initiatives, notably by King Hussein of Jordan, to reach a similar accommodation with the government of Israel. Such an important and stabilising element as the government of Egypt was removed in the 1980s. Any sense of growing security and balance in international politics was seriously disrupted, and this was the essential reality with which governments had to contend after 1980.

No statesman ignored the changes. Most of the principal leaders were also new, often brought into office unexpectedly. Only the USA and the United Kingdom among western states, retained a consistent leadership. During the years of Mr Reagan's presidency the Soviet Union saw four different political leaders—Leonid Brezhnev, the brief periods of Mr Andropov and Mr Chernenko, and Mr Gorbachev. Such a reversal of the more familiar pattern of Soviet political stability and American electoral swings invited new assessments of policy and balance. The changes afforded an unprecedented opportunity, with both sides released from the burden of entrenched positions and commitments. But other significant personalities disappeared and were replaced by leaders whose stamp required careful measurement. President Sadat of

Egypt and Helmut Schmidt of the Federal Republic of Germany had both created policies of international importance, but were no longer present to lead the world; President Sadat was assassinated in 1982 and Helmut Schmidt defeated in elections lacking support for his policies from within his own Social Democratic Party. Political defeat or assassination also removed Menachem Begin, Mrs Indira Ghandi, and President Valéry Giscard d'Estaing of France. For the first time the French state was in the hands of the socialists after the presidential and legislative elections of 1981. But in all of this the impact was less dramatic than had been anticipated in some quarters. Although the French Communist Party was a coalition partner with the French socialists from the election in 1981 until August 1984, few major changes of policy were perceived. Foreign policy retained a Gaullist flavour—some wits even suggested that President Mitterrand had begun to look like Charles de Gaulle, if lacking something of his stature. France continued its important role in Africa, the leader of the many states which had emerged from the French Empire.

Within five months of becoming President, Mitterrand called for an African international force to intervene in the civil war in Chad where the armed units of Goukouni Oueddi were assisted by Libyan air and armoured support against the administration of Hissene Habre. By August 1983, the French had launched 'operation Manta', with 3000 French troops occupying the centre of the country. Such policies, continuing into 1986, were consistent with the earlier military interventions which went back to 1969. The socialist government also continued the strong defence policies associated with presidents of the centre-right—an independent nuclear force, research programmes into new weapons, and substantial arms production and sales. There were new policies too, notably the support given by the French government to the Sandinista government which had come to power in Nicaragua in 1979.[1] Yet the major change in government in this important European state had less impact than the uncertainties which followed the shifts in Soviet leadership.

The successive deaths of three General Secretaries of the Soviet Communist Party between 1982 and 1985 brought many new faces to Soviet politics. In international relations many questions were asked when a younger man assumed the senior political responsibilities of the Soviet Union. Mr Gorbachev invited a radical review of policies. He was able to present a forceful and effective public image. His handling of the journalists of the world was a new departure for the Soviet leadership, and he used these media for policy statements, such as the series of propositions about arms limitation, made in 1985 and 1986. With such new faces and approaches, a fresh and quizzical look was taken at Soviet policy. As if to reinforce the extent of the changes, Andrei Gromyko retired from his position as Foreign Minister, to become President of the Soviet Union, thereby bringing an entire epoch in international relations to an end. He had been at the centre of international events since before the Second World War. His experience was without parallel. In 1985, he had gone from the world of diplomacy, but the extent of real changes in the policies of the USSR remained limited.

In 1985 the Soviet delegation returned to the Geneva arms limitations negotiations. The military build-up of land and sea forces had continued, as did the search for secure bases. By the 1980s, the Soviet Union had a presence—diplomatic and often naval—in the Indian Ocean and South-East Asia, in the waters of the Red Sea and on the African continent. Soviet submarines were tracked all over the globe, even within the American hemisphere and the Antarctic. In the 1980s, the Soviet Union manufactured or granted manufacturing rights for a high proportion of the world's weaponry. Some 80 per cent of the automatic weapons produced were of Soviet design and manufacture.[2] All states had to assess this power and the heaviest responsibilities fell upon the administration of the United States of America.

President Reagan expressed a wish to 'build a safer world', and, like him or not, he placed a distinctive mark on the policies of the USA. Election to a second term as President in 1984 gave him an authority that none of his predecessors in the 1970s had possessed. None had achieved this. The appearance of an intellectual lightweight, apparently confirmed by the occasional tactless remark, had to be reconciled with President Reagan's undoubted popularity and tremendous skill before the American public. He could capture a mood and conduct public emotions with confidence. His curious suggestion that a limited nuclear war might be fought in Europe had to be set against his successful determination to get the Soviet leaders to face up to new realities, to come to talk about the military and political developments of the 1980s. The ability—or perhaps it was fortune—that enabled his administration to bring down levels of unemployment in the United States and to sustain economic growth in many sectors, was linked to a policy of a strong dollar, which only showed signs of failing in 1986. Moreover, the military strength of the United States was greater than at any time since the Vietnam War, and its international political significance was equally assertive. President Reagan could not be ignored. He was the single most important person in international politics in 1986 as he was in 1981. Despite many predictions that his words would be followed by forceful and dangerous policies, even by war, the United States was not at war. No major campaign had been initiated whether in the Middle East or in Central America. The marines and the American rapid deployment forces remain in their bases and ships.

Moreover the deceptive familiarity of international relations was affected by other quite new developments. Had the balance of forces between the Soviet Union and the United States actually shifted? Suspicions were voiced in the USA before 1980 that the Soviet Union had been able to gain a significant military and political advantage. The expansion of Soviet forces and the spread of Soviet influence, particularly in Africa, in Nicaragua and in the evident Soviet determination to remain politically dominant in Afghanistan, were all noted. The production and deployment of new Soviet weapons, particularly nuclear weapons, encouraged these suspicions, and gave them substance. By 1980 the government of the United States had to accept the reality of Soviet power and the seeming loss of superiority. The nuclear arms of the Soviet Union and the military balance were the main focus of the argument about superiority and the relative increase in power and influence. Armaments were assumed to be the measure of power. In the 1980s, this became a misleading assumption, although it remained popular and widely attractive.

However this view was more apparent than real, and the nature of superpower strength changed most significantly with technical developments. Political developments have always been linked to the evolution of technology. Organisation and the processes of production fundamentally alter the capacity of states to play a part in international relations. This has been at the heart of politics since the emergence of states in the late Middle Ages, when Machiavelli confronted the advent of artillery and got it wrong—guns would never make an impact, he argued.[3] In the 1980s, the impact of technical change in manufacturing suggests a deep transformation of the balance of power and the relationships between states. The ability to produce in volume within a shorter time after research and development is the crucial new element. The accelerating rate of change in the research and production of new ideas and new equipment has been to the advantage of the United States and its allies. The administration in Washington has demonstrated a willingness to grasp this important feature of the contemporary world. Undoubtedly other states had the capacity to match the technology, including the Soviet Union. The production techniques and innovations could be developed or purchased. But, as the Second World War revealed, the productive capacity of the United States over an almost inconceivable range of goods has been virtually unchallenged. Only Japan has shown the organisation and management skills needed to match American dynamism in moving from research, through development to production. In the 1980s the projected production life of the most advanced electrical equipment dropped below ten years, and in some cases was considerably shorter. In the manufacture of lasers, compact discs, robots, teleprinters and the telecommunication industries, the presuppositions of a few years ago have been cast aside. Together with this vastly accelerated rate of change have come quite different production criteria. Quality controls in some of these and related industries have had to accept up to 90 per cent failure and rejection rates. Old views about manufacturing have had to be abandoned. The sensitivity of equipment and the scale of production imposed hitherto unknown standards, unthinkable to the manufacturers of motor cars, car parts, railways and ships in previous epochs.

New production techniques have become essential for the manufacture and maintenance of new weapons and techniques of war.

At least Machiavelli was correct when he argued that organisation was more important than a flash of inspiration and innovation. Adolf Hitler committed the opposite error; he placed too much confidence in novelty, and production difficulties bedevilled the German rocket programme. The balance between organisation and innovation has never been easy to perceive. In 1985 the leaders of the USA and the USSR were both looking in a similar direction. The need was for such states to come to terms with the technical changes of the last decades of the twentieth century. Mr Gorbachev spoke of the need to improve efficiency in Soviet organisation; President Reagan invested millions of dollars in innovative programmes, including that for the strategic defence initiative, generally dubbed the 'star wars' programme.

Many different pressures are exerted upon the superpowers in the 1980s. The possibility of sustaining the category of 'superpower' has been called into question. The following chapters are concerned with these issues. They conclude with the need to recognise the position of influence that is still held by the United States of America in international politics. The assessment of that position determines the rest of any analysis of international relations. Criticism of the USA focuses on the ability of its government to exert political and military force.

The 'ability' of the government in Washington is a combination of will and freedom of action. After 1981 there was little question of that will. The administration of President Reagan adopted a strong policy in all respects. That did not necessarily mean direct action, although this also was taken on a number of occasions—in the Caribbean, in the Lebanon and against Libya. The availability of units equipped and trained for fast, very manoeuvrable, short-term attack was significant. These were the troops, with air support, that were used—the development of the rapid deployment force introduced by the previous administration. However there were constraints on the will of government. The impact of the war in Vietnam and the need to withdraw without victory caused a general criticism of policies. The result was a revision of the relationship between President and Congress which persisted in the following decade.

President Reagan found himself hemmed in by Congressional powers and the subject of close strutiny. The War Powers Act 1972 was the heart of the new relationship. The President was required to explain policy and action within thirty days of his decision if troops were committed. A short extension could be granted, up to ninety days. The principle was clear; involvement was dependent on the mood and approval of Congress. Quick action was made more difficult, and secrecy was also difficult because Congressional committees were to be kept fully informed, including on matters relating to United States agents and intelligence operations. Transfers of funds from one heading in the defence budget to another item were also excluded in this post-Vietnam legislation. Such transfers can only take place with Congressional approval. Military aid and other assistance, especially of vital equipment and resources, are all carefully scrutinised. Military aid to Laos and Kampuchea was cut in 1974, as was that to Turkey in 1974 and to the anti-government UNITA forces fighting in Angola in 1975. These measures bedevilled President Reagan's policies in Central America. Congress stopped military aid for the anti-government Contra forces in Nicaragua in 1984–86, preferring to allow only non-military materials, medical supplies, food and clothing. Although it was always hard to ensure that such restrictions were obeyed, presidential discretion had gone.

In 1977 Congress introduced another criterion in assessing the dispatch of American aid. Were the potential recipients conforming to acceptable standards of human rights? No regimes or groups could automatically expect aid without satisfying this criterion. The idea was by no means new. In 1961, aid had been made conditional on progress towards democracy for regimes in Latin America. Again there were problems in monitoring and applying such criteria. In the 1980s the limitation on executive action was particularly awkward since performance on matters of human rights might vary greatly from place to place, and from year to year (even from month to month). The result was that in El Salvador, for example, the representatives of the government of the United

States, usually the Secretary of State himself, spent the years 1982–86 urging more unequivocal compliance with acceptable standards in order to guide presidential measures through Congress. The paths for decisive presidential action in foreign and defence policy were not smooth. Missile programmes were reversed, aid policy was checked, and intelligence operations hampered in the years 1981–86, despite the wide public support for President Reagan and his desire to restore United States self-respect.

Before 1981 and the change to the Republican administration, there had been assertions that these many limitations and restrictions on executive action had contributed to a serious loss of influence for the USA. In contrast, the Soviet Union was thought to have grasped the opportunity to maximise its influence. However during the 1980s this suspicion was shown to have been exaggerated in a number of important respects. It was true that there were new and more Soviet missiles, and that military build-up had occurred or continued. But the political influence was less than the more pessimistic observers in the United States suggested. The Cubans, strongly present in southern Africa, were conducting a policy as much their own as Soviet. Castro had stressed the Afro-Cuban link which, with its racial overtones, limited Soviet influence precisely because it was essentially European. Soviet intervention was cautious in the Middle East despite an important ally in the government in Damascus. Soviet influence was unsure. Their officials were present in South Yemen and Libya, but in the 1980s were seen to have limited influence on policy. Local and short-term factors were revealed to have as much bearing on events as the pressure of superpower interests. The awesome implications of involving the superpowers threatened all governments. The limits of the influence of the United States were less certain and hence the foreign policy of the government of the United States was more vulnerable.[4] The support of the United States for this or that regime brought risks. The option was to minimise those risks and to increase the ability to take independent action. In many ways this was the direction that Soviet policy had taken. A growing navy, military production and supply afforded the possibility for more independent policy. The expansion of

Soviet action, political and military, since the early 1970s, required the corresponding freeing of United States policy from the constraints of earlier, more rigid policies, tied to particular governments and states. The USA and USSR therefore brought their foreign and defence policies into realignment. The suspected spread of Soviet influence into all continents and oceans required a readjustment of American policy.

In the eighteenth century Jean-Jacques Rousseau reminded his readers that states had to compare themselves in order to know themselves, to compare their power to that of other states in order to assess their own strength.[5] The effects of this readjustment in the 1980s were felt in the development of Soviet–American relations.

NOTES

1. The French government had provided trucks, two patrol boats and two helicopters in 1981, according to the press of the time. Total sales, including rockets, were quoted as being as much as $15.8 million.
2. Kalachnikov automatic weapons were manufactured in several states, many in the Middle East, in Eastern Europe and Yugoslavia, and in the People's Republic of China. Further information provided to the author by an arms manufacturer. See also Jane's *Infantry Weapons*.
3. *The Discourses,* Book 2, section 17; 'In what esteem artillery should be held by armies at the present time and whether the opinion universally held in its regard is sound'.
4. 'As America entered the 1980s she was richer and more powerful—and more vulnerable—than at any time in her history' (S.E. Ambrose, *Rise to Globalism,* 3rd edn, Penguin Books, London, 1983, p. 21).
5. 'Thus the size of the body politic being purely relative, it is forced to compare itself in order to know itself; it depends on its whole environment and has to take an interest in all that happens' (Rousseau, 'The State of War', quoted in M.G. Forsyth *et al., The Theory of International Relations,* Allen & Unwin, London, 1970, p. 17).

1 Superpower Equivalence

The history of international relations since 1945 contained a simple message: The world had to accept the primacy of two states, the nuclear giants, the United States of America and the Soviet Union. By 1970 or thereabouts their influence was felt everywhere, their navies roamed the oceans from Antarctica to the Bering Strait and the North Atlantic, their weapons and expertise were found in all continents. Survival of the race itself seemed to rest in their governments' hands. A process, begun during the closing stages of the Second World War, had come to fruition. But this was deceptive. The nature and extent of the deception became clearer during the 1980s and herein lay the importance of these years.

These two great states were no less mighty in 1980. Although both India and China had larger populations and had resolved some of the desperate weaknesses of earlier years, they had fewer tanks and aircraft, their industrial output was relatively meagre and their exploitation of diverse energy resources, including nuclear energy, was feebler than was the case with the two 'superpowers'. The eyes of the world were on Geneva in November 1985 when the leaders of the Soviet Union and the United States met, with the level of interest comparable to the conferences of Yalta and Potsdam in 1945, or Vienna 1961 when President Kennedy met Mr Khrushchev. Other intervening conferences had not perhaps attracted such a degree of keen expectation. But something in the nature of Soviet–American relations had changed, and that change was already underway by 1980.

The central element in the changed relationship between the

Soviet Union and the United States concerns the place of the military balance. This acquired a new, or at least a different, political importance. Although the military balance between the forces on both sides of the Iron Curtain has absorbed attention since the end of the Second World War, the military strength has been presented as an integral part of the overall political strength. The USSR has placed its troops where its interest and influence require them, where its ideological mouth is. The same is true of the United States. Whether a mistaken interest was occasionally perceived is not the crucial point. The formula is the indivisibility of superpower strength in all its many aspects—military, economic and political. However in the period after détente and perhaps because of détente, the consideration of the military balance was disentangled from the wider factors. A military balance between the superpowers might be considered quite separately from the recognition of spheres of interest or the competition for influence, and the division of the world into two camps. The effect was that good relations were sought for special aims, particularly for military needs. These relations therefore survived the series of quite dramatic events that threatened the bilateral discussion and diplomatic contact during the 1980s. In addition, there was a vital political point which demanded definition and exploration of its implications. This was the nature of superpower parity or equivalence. What this meant and how this affected diplomacy and tensions was never completely agreed.

The relations between the two governments were based on tension, the mutual suspicions of deterrence. A kind of oscillation between good times and bad formed the basis of the analysis of Cold War and détente. The evolution of détente became natural and logical. What more natural than a drift back to Cold War with renewed tensions and military competition? This transition appeared to have happened by 1980. The Soviet Union had apparently increased its armoury, both nuclear and conventional. By 1979 the NATO assessment was that 880 nuclear warheads gave the Soviet Union superiority in intermediate range weapons. The result was the decision taken by the NATO Foreign and Defence Ministers in Brussels, on 12 December 1979, to modernise the alliance's intermediate range missiles. The intention was to deploy 108 Pershing II launchers and 464 ground-launched cruise missiles in the United Kingdom, West Germany, Italy, the Netherlands and Belgium. Simultaneously, an effort was to be made to negotiate an arms control agreement with the Soviet Union. This was consistent with the policy familiar to NATO members and enunciated in the Harmel Report 1967: the carrot and the stick, the safeguarding of security through defence efforts and the seeking of arms control agreements.

Within days of the so-called twin-track decision taken in Brussels, the Soviet Union invaded Afghanistan. This campaign, ostensibly in support of the Marxist regime there under threat from 'subversive elements', appeared to confirm the renewed Cold War atmosphere. The government of the United States and many others expressed surprise and disapproval. This was perhaps a wise and cautious reaction. Any public admission of prior knowledge might have required more positive action on the part of the United States government which had recently begun to express concern about the extent of Soviet influence in many Third World states. During the years after withdrawal of American troops from Vietnam, Soviet influence was perceived in South-East Asia, in the newly independent states of Angola and Mozambique, and in many parts of the Middle East. The election of Ronald Reagan to the presidency in 1980 heightened the sense of deteriorating relations between the United States and the Soviet Union. His predecessor, Jimmy Carter, became associated for many, both inside the country and elsewhere, with too lenient an approach, and too great an assertion of human rights issues. Even the diplomatic triumph of his presidency—the bringing together of President Sadat and Mr Begin, the political leaders of Egypt and Israel at Camp David—smacked of a ready optimism about international politics. The increase in the defence budgets from 1977 and the investment in researching new systems of weapons were forgotten.

Therefore, by 1980, fear of significant new tension between the USSR and the USA was widespread. Here was a new Cold War or a second Cold War, even a new international order. On further inspection these 'new' conditions were found to be reconstructions of the old Cold War, although more menacing. The more guarded 'new realism' of the Rt Hon Dr David Owen, expounded in a speech in October 1983, was much the same. There was a narrowness about many of these discussions. They were variations of the original theme, albeit 'much more threatening than the old Cold War of the 1950's.[1] The 'New Realism', despite the dialectical analysis of the interplay between 'competition and cooperation inherent in détente',[2] turned out to be more of the same—further cooperation and negotiation, punctuated by periods of tension. In contrast, the drift towards 'globalism' by the United States was only a restatement of an old theme; 'the Cold War continued, more expensive and more dangerous than ever'.[3] But the comparison between Soviet–American relations in the 1980s and the earlier phases of the Cold War lacked conviction as the decade proceeded. The atmosphere differed essentially from the bitter and silent years of the earlier Cold War. Stalinism, the rhetoric of Senator Joseph McCarthy and the sharp clash of communism and democracy lacked the basic elements of international political order. There were few points of contact and regular relations were constantly interrupted by suspicion and by the failure to establish more than a veneer of permanent diplomatic communication. In previous examples of great power conflict there had always been diplomacy and regular politics; indeed conflict had been measured through the diplomatic tensions. E.H. Carr's famous account of *Twenty Years' Crisis*—the confrontation between realism and idealism in the years 1919–39—was a study in international *relations*. This was nothing like the empty dialogue of 1947–53. After the origins of the Cold War and the early formulation, relations between the two victors of 1945 improved and became permanent. In the 1980s despite all the fears and the talk of renewed Cold War, Soviet–American contacts remained open, and herein lay the difference.

The governments of the United States and the Soviet Union had opened a new era of their contacts with the brief meetings of the war years, from 1943 to 1945. The basis of that contact was cemented by the spasmodic correspondence between President Roosevelt and Marshal Stalin, involving the stormy personality of Winston Churchill as a kind of intermediary.

These peculiar beginnings culminated in the Cold War years, two powerfully armed states confronting each other, supported by exhausted and dependent allies. These years of Cold War created a bipolarity that was finally recognised in the policies of Dr Henry Kissinger. Détente was only fully possible once bipolarity had been accepted. But once a lessening of tension had been achieved, a new direction was anticipated in Soviet–American relations, and after 1980 the dualism took on a new complexion. Thus although the relationship between the United States and the USSR dominated international politics no less in the 1980s than in earlier years, something was different, and no such simple formula as Cold War or détente sufficed. Uncertainty became the hallmark of the years 1980–85. Each speech and each event threatened to shift the balance from fear of increased hostility between the USA and the USSR to new hopes of peaceful cooperation.

However regular relations continued, although no meeting between an American President and a Soviet leader occurred after the Vienna summit of June 1979, when President Carter and Mr Brezhnev signed the second Strategic Arms Limitation Treaty until November 1985. This meeting and the continuing contacts of these years seemed all the more remarkable in view of the events which strained relations between 1979 and 1985. At times the rhetoric was harsh. Soviet press comment and public statements denounced the policies of the United States. These attacks concentrated upon Europe, Central America and the Middle East. In Nicaragua the arming of the opposition forces, the Contras, enabled them to continue the civil war against the Sandinista government. Further arming of the Egyptian forces was also 'destabilising'.[4] The United States had 'deliberately wrecked the Geneva talks' on the limitation of nuclear weapons.[5] The Soviet view of United States policies was highly critical:

There is no escaping the reality of nuclear confrontation by following the road of developing ever new means of destruction, including the space-based 'superweapons'. This is a reference to the plans for installing a 'space-shield' which would protect against a retaliatory strike. This 'shield' would serve the aggressive policy of US imperialism. What is meant is measures constituting part of a general offensive plan intended for upsetting the strategic parity, gaining military superiority and preparing for a first nuclear strike in the hope of getting away with it unscathed.[6]

For his part President Reagan fulminated against the 'evil empire' of the Soviet Union, in a speech given in Florida in March 1983. He also opposed Soviet actions in Afghanistan and their possible actions in Poland. The President suggested that relations might improve 'if the Soviet Union revealed that it is willing to moderate its imperialism, its aggression'.[7] In 1983 the Institute of Strategic Studies in London concluded that 'Soviet—American relations in 1983 deteriorated to their lowest point in over twenty years'.[8] However the stresses created by some of the events which occurred between 1979 and 1985 caused only short-lived tensions.

The Soviet military offensive into Afghanistan which began in December 1979 and continues over seven years later, had been the largest operation undertaken by the Soviet Union since 1945. The denunciation of the operation suggested a stormy decade for the 1980s. The United States failed to attend the Olympic Games in Moscow in 1980. The USSR and most other communist states boycotted the Games in Los Angeles in 1984. But the USA drew some satisfaction from the Soviet military campaign. The USSR could no longer enjoy the luxury of righteousness as in the years of the involvement of the United States in the war in Vietnam. But superpower relations did not invite complacency; in 1983, the United States used its troops to overthrow an unconstitutional regime in the Caribbean island of Grenada. A brief campaign saw the expulsion of the Marxist faction that had taken power, and of their Cuban 'advisers'. A constitutional regime was established. Although this operation was on a tiny scale in comparison to that of the Soviet Union in Afghanistan, criticism was levelled at a great state that had intervened in the politics of a small and weak one. The Grenadan operation began to acquire something of the stigma of the United States intervention in 1965 in the Dominican Republic. Yet in 1983, the American troops, assisted by those of other Caribbean states, swiftly and successfully removed an administration that had butchered the previous political leader, Mr Bishop, and restored such stable rule that Queen Elizabeth was able to make a state visit to Grenada in 1985.

Whilst such military actions sharpened mutual criticism, US—Soviet relations were not spoiled. They survived other incidents. In August 1983, an American senator and 268 other people were killed when a South Korean Boeing 747 airliner was shot down by Soviet fighters, defending their airspace. The Boeing had apparently drifted off course. Publicity and bitter recriminations followed, but the drama passed. In February 1985, an American army officer, Major Nicholson, was shot and killed by a Russian sentry. The American officer had been taking photographs of material regarded as 'restricted', although outside the agreed 'restricted area' at the time. The incident was an embarrassment for both the USSR and the USA at a time when better relations were sought and some ambiguity surrounded the events; what was being photographed? had the sentry, probably a conscript, acted too hastily? The Americans admitted that Major Nicholson had been 'observing tank sheds'. This was an incident that might have been expected to have soured relations most severely. The shooting occurred in the German Democratic Republic, and the officer was on duty at the time, a member of the United States military mission. Agreements made at the end of the Second World War, permitted all allied military commands, the British, French, Soviet and American, to have access to each others' zones of occupation. The position remained unchanged despite the creation of the two German states, and Major Nicholson was engaged on such an official tour. These duties afforded opportunities to observe and to investigate. Thus the death of an officer and the suspicions surrounding his activities, allegedly in a restricted area, was a potentially very serious episode. There were perhaps dim recollections of the U-2 'spy'plane' shot down over Soviet territory in 1960. But in 1985, there was no deterioration in Soviet–American relations. What emerged was the determination to prevent such a slide. Daily relations between Soviet and United States army officers and officials were reported to have remained friendly and cooperative.

After the Carter–Brezhnev meeting in 1979, a further summit was expected. In 1981 journalists pestered President Reagan about the possibility of such an encounter. The expectation was there. The nervous jostling of the first meeting, those of President Eisenhower and Mr Khrushchev at Camp David, President Kennedy and Mr Khrushchev at Vienna and the meeting between President Johnson and Mr

Kosygin at Glassborough, USA, in 1967, had given place to more constructive encounters. Positive results were expected, not merely symbolic confrontations. President Nixon met Mr Brezhnev three times between May 1972 and July 1974. President Ford met the same Soviet leader in November 1974 at Vladivostok. Therefore a great burden of hopes was placed upon the new leaders; President Reagan was confident and resilient, and Mr Gorbachev exploited his relatively youthful image, reminiscent of the vigour of Kennedy. President Reagan needed a substantial agreement in order to justify a meeting with the Soviet leader and continue the harmonious process initiated by President Nixon.

But in the 1980s it was clear that Soviet–United States relations did not consist solely nor principally of summit diplomacy. It did not depend upon the vagaries of an incidental event, unanticipated by leaders in either Moscow or Washington. Regular relations were never interrupted between the 1979 summit and that of November 1985. The meeting between President Reagan and Mr Gorbachev was the climax of a series of meetings as much as a departure and a turning-point for the future. The basis of established contacts had been laid during the years of détente and was not destroyed despite the invasions of Afghanistan and Grenada. These events were recognised by both sides as secondary to the main business of developing good relations.

The points of contact between the Soviet Union and the United States were greater in number in the 1980s than before. They met in many formal settings, at United Nations committees and plenary sessions, in the almost anachronistic world of West Berlin and some other relics of 1945 in Europe. Their delegates were in session at Geneva for arms talks, and in Vienna for force reduction talks. The issues of the oceans, the polar regions and space brought Russians and Americans together. The subjects of these Soviet and American meetings were also more specific. This applied particularly to the many meetings involving weapons, and in the 1980s the focal point for these talks was Geneva. Detailed matters had been considered in the 1970s. The first agreement on strategic arms control, the SALT 1 treaty, signed in 1972, had specified precise numbers for missiles launchers. The agreement had also recognised that both sides might increase their missile strength and fixed limits were stated in the provisions. The provisions also stated the precise numbers of modern ballistic missile submarines that both states were to be permitted—44 in the case of the USA and 62 for the Soviet Union. The issue of nuclear weapons and their limitation had been in abeyance since 1979. Despite a signed treaty between the Soviet and American governments, known as SALT 2, Congress failed to ratify it. The governments had more or less adhered to the provisions although there was no treaty, ratified and lodged with the United Nations. The basis of future detailed discussion on arms control was therefore not lost, but merely in suspension.

However public attention had not been diverted. Concern over the development of new weapons had been aroused in 1977. Radiation weapons seemed to go beyond the firm agreements between the United States and the Soviet Union. A now notorious article in the *Washington Post* in 1977 made clear that money had been voted and spent on the development of an enhanced radiation bomb, a neutron bomb. This weapon was capable of destroying people rather than property, the ultimate 'capitalist' weapon. Misconceptions about the performance and the deployment did not stop public concern. There was particular worry in Europe, and especially in the Federal Republic of Germany, because the weapon might be appropriately used in Europe. The neutron bomb panic was an important element in the revitalised peace movements in West Europe. But the public was concerned about all types of new weapons and indeed about the overall build-up of weapons. The careful statistical approach of the drafters of the SALT treaties merely played into the hands of the peace and anti-nuclear protesters; arms control envisaged an increase in numbers of weapons, and did not bother with new types of weapon. The concentration on weapons, new and old, lifted the issue out of the argument about class and economic system, about Soviet against American interests. It was a humanitarian argument. Into this debate came the communiqué from the NATO Foreign Ministers of 12 December, 1979. The special meeting held in Brussels decided that the cruise and Pershing 2 intermediate-range missiles were to be installed in American bases in Western Europe. The initial deployment was to be deferred until late 1983. This decision received condemnation from the Soviet Union and from political personalities and some political parties in all the host states. Public protest in 1982–84 was widespread. Arms became a dominant public issue.

By the time that President Reagan took over the administration in 1981, arms control had become 'the barometer of the superpower relationship'.[9] The Soviet Union and public protest, especially in Federal Germany, focused attention on the issue of arms control and limitation. Moreover, the refusal of the United States Congress to endorse the agreement made by President Carter and Mr Brezhnev, kept nuclear arms control a vital matter. The United States and the Soviet Union were judged by the willingness of their governments to agree to arms limitations and controls. A series of public 'offers' was begun in 1982, when Mr Brezhnev pronounced a unilateral Soviet moratorium on long-range weapons. The ebb and flow of proposals for consideration continued through the 1980s. In this atmosphere the attention of the world moved away from the normal discourse of states. While Soviet and American representatives met in many places to carry out official functions in embassies, at the United Nations and in the many agencies in which their governments participated, Cold War or détente was measured by performance in arms negotiations. The dates and procedures were already set for future talks. All manner of obligations had been created in the period of détente. The expectation was encouraged that the momentum would be sustained. Thus among all the US–Soviet contacts, arms discussions achieved a prominence.

Other political meetings between East and West were also affected. It was not surprising that the multinational talks on European security narrowed their focus through the 1980s. The broad-based conference on security and cooperation in Europe which had first met at Helsinki in 1975, considered many social and economic matters. Although these were on the agenda of subsequent meetings, attention drifted away from such CSCE gatherings and moved to Geneva and arms negotiations in the 1980s. The security and cooperation agenda became slower to complete. After a first review of the working of the CSCE procedures, at Belgrade in 1977–78, it took three years to complete the second review at Madrid. From 1980 until September 1983, delegates debated an agenda, the allegations about violations of previous agreements, and also future projects. Even this progress was dramatically interrupted by events in Poland.

The imposition of martial law in Poland was followed in October 1981 by the outlawing of the workers' union organisation, known as Solidarity. The controls imposed on economic and social freedom in Poland by the new government of General Jaruzelski went to the heart of the Helsinki agreements. Argument and complaint delayed progress in Madrid, as did the coincidence that the session at which these issues were debated early in 1982, was under the authority of a Polish chairman.[10] The West European delegations and those of the United States and the neutral and non-aligned states fulminated at the Polish policies. But the Polish government managed to keep control, despite demonstrations. Restrictions placed upon the leader of Solidarity, Mr Lech Walesa, and the removal by the government of the United States of 'most favoured nation' status for Poland, following the ban on Solidarity, were weathered by General Jaruzelski. His rule was made secure without overt Soviet intervention. By the end of the Madrid conference, Poland was no longer a central issue. The Helsinki agreements and proposals had been flouted without sanction of any serious kind. Arms control and matters military had resumed their place. The final document of the Madrid review meeting suggested future conferences and above all proposed a conference on disarmament in Europe.

The focus on arms limitation and control moved to Stockholm in 1984. The Conference on disarmament in Europe was regional, involving the 35 states that had participated at Helsinki in 1975. The subject was conventional weapons and the date for the opening session was January 1984. Thus the military interests of the European states, including the neutral and non-aligned states, took pre-eminence over the other matters raised at the original Helsinki conference. Although there were discussions about economic, cultural and scientific exchange, about human rights (these being the contents of the other two 'baskets' of measures presented at Helsinki), the Stockholm agenda concerned confidence and security-building measures.[11] Other issues were left for future meetings, the follow-up conference to be held in Vienna in 1986.

While the Helsinki process dragged on through the years after the Soviet invasion of Afghanistan and the tensions in Poland, another regular meeting-place brought the USA and the Soviet Union to the same table. It was always through the elegant capitals and major cities of Europe that the delegations moved, carrying the fate of the world in their suitcases, from Helsinki to Belgrade and Madrid, from Berne to Vienna. In the last of these cities the two military alliances, NATO and the Warsaw Pact, had faced each other since 1973. The Mutual and Balanced Force Reduction Talks, or as some NATO wags would have it, the 'More benefit for the Russians talks', seemed to have brought little obvious result. However, this was to miss the significant point. The many arguments and proposals, the draft treaties submitted by both sides, from NATO in July 1982 and from the Warsaw Pact in February 1983, showed a narrowing of differences. Equal ceilings, after troop reductions, and a clearer and agreed definition of what constituted 'troops', were put forward for the central front in Europe. Both sides accepted that the withdrawing of Soviet and American forces was to be the first step in the balanced force reductions. This point was reached in the 1980s after long and cautious negotiation. In short, the principle of parity between the two military groupings and between the USA and the USSR was explicitly recognised at Vienna.

But these meetings took second place in the 1980s. In arms control, as in many other international matters, all roads led to Geneva. In that city the USA and the USSR kept negotiations alive, despite interruptions and some ill-feeling. The basis of the discussions was parity. This had acquired two aspects. The achievement of parity was partly directed at numbers—numbers of systems and numbers of war-heads. This was not an easy matter in itself, and comparability confused the goal of parity. But parity was also a principle. This became a much more serious political issue during the

1980s and worked in the interests of the Soviet Union. The principle of parity between the Soviet Union and the United States had been implicit for many years. It was certainly implied in the SALT 1 treaty of 1972. The principle was clearly stated in the agreement of 1979 between the two leaders, and parity in numbers was proposed, covering specific categories of launchers. Although this SALT 2 agreement did not cover other types of weapon, particularly the most recent developments of cruise missiles, some multiple and independently targeted rockets, and warheads fired from the same first-stage of a missile (MIRVs), the crucial principle, that of parity, was introduced into the agreement and draft treaty.[12]

At first there was disillusionment. The Soviet Union faced the prospect of new weapons in Europe which were not covered by the agreement (which had not been ratified by Congress, in any case). High-speed, accurate missiles as well as low-level cruise missiles were to be deployed, all capable of reaching Soviet territory. This was decided in December 1979, by the NATO Foreign and Defence Ministers. Defence against such missiles was likely to be very costly, in particular requiring new vertical radar systems of the AWACS type, already developed by the USA. Equally powerful was the disappointment of Europeans, especially on the part of those who were aware of the deployment of new Soviet intermediate range missiles, the SS 20s. These were regarded as indications of a breach of faith, altering the very basis of the agreement between the governments of the Soviet Union and the United States. Although Congress had not ratified the SALT 2 treaty, the broad understanding had been that both sides adhered to the agreement. By 1980 and 1981, this understanding was shattered. The replacement of older SS 4 and SS 5 missiles by the more advanced SS 20 appeared to make nonsense of the principle of parity. These weapons were 'a significant improvement over previous systems in providing greater accuracy, more mobility and greater range as well as having multiple warheads'.[13] However, the NATO decision to deploy new American weapons went hand in hand with a determination to begin new negotiations. These duly took place in Geneva in the autumn of 1980. Full discussions began a year later once the new administration had taken office in Washington. The Soviet Foreign Minister, Mr Gromyko, and the Secretary of State, General Haig, initiated these talks. Their impact was to be felt through the next years. They dominated relations between the two states.

The development of negotiating positions suggested two levels of difficulties. The USSR was reluctant to abandon an initial advantage, gained through the installation of SS 20s. The United States urged parity. Thus a moratorium was rejected by the government of the United States. A unilateral 'freeze' at existing levels in 1982, announced by Mr Brezhnev, was denounced in Washington and Bonn as fraudulent.[14] No halt to deployment had been called. The Soviet Union suggested on several occasions that British and French weapons should be included in any negotiation, and form part of an agreed parity among the nuclear states. This would also have left the Soviet Union with an advantage over the European states, but there was little prospect in the years 1982–85 that the western governments would agree. All manner of political difficulties faced such a proposal, not least the relative advantage for the governments of France and Britain, neither of which could really accept a subordinate role in Europe. However disagreements over performance and verification made any chance of a formal negotiation covering nuclear weapons in Europe impossible to achieve before December 1983, when the new missiles began to be deployed and the government of the USSR left the Geneva talks. Although the Soviet Union returned its delegation to Geneva, no agreement had been signed with the USA when the two leaders met in November 1985.

Yet beneath the agony and uncertainty was the fact that negotiations had more or less continued since 1979. The interruptions were brief. The range of talks included the Strategic Arms Reduction Talks (the so-called START process). The central theme was parity, the political significance of which became greater as the decade progressed. The USA proposed parity, but progress in negotiation was slow. The Soviet Union urged the inclusion of intermediate range weapons which could also reach Soviet territory. Into the 1980s, therefore, came concrete proposals for superpower agreement. The West German Defence White Paper of 1983 observed that 'even in the present overall situation in the political sphere agreements between West and East are feasible'.[15] The crucial point was that the basis of the talks was parity. The argument about parity affected not merely weapons, but the very nature of US–Soviet relations. The years 1979–85 were thus totally different from any previous phase of their relationship.

Many noted the issue of 'superiority' as an aspect in the arms control negotiations. The Soviet Union, among others, decried the apparent reluctance on the part of the government of the USA to accept the loss of 'superiority'. In the United States, there had been some stress on what were seen as attempts by the Soviet Union to acquire 'superiority'. In the case of intermediate-range nuclear missiles in Europe, the USSR appeared to have achieved this advantage by 1979. Both states stressed parity. However there was no easy way in which Russians and Americans could agree on the definition of parity. They held substantially different points of view before and during the 1980s.

Equivalence or parity for the government of the USA had to be a limited matter, excluding economic and moral issues. No United States government could readily accept that the USSR had equivalence in economic potential. The achievement of a socialist economic performance which could match that of a democratic and free market state would undermine the moral and political position held by the USA and its allies. There was therefore little room for agreement on parity in this sense. Nor could the American conception of freedom as a principle of politics be easily reconciled to the view of a totalitarian world in the Soviet Union. No American acceptance of parity in this sphere could be expected. For the governments of the USA equivalence had to remain a limited matter, confined to the balance of the arsenals of the two superpowers.

Matters were viewed rather differently from the USSR. There had been a clear understanding that it was hard to achieve a general recognition of parity, but this remained the aim: a demonstration that Soviet economic and moral policies and values were the equal of those of the USA. For the Soviet Union the area of arms control and agreement offered the broadest path towards a wider equality. Military balance on the basis of parity in numbers had attractions for both sides. In a sense their interests were the same. The security of all was enhanced by agreement and balance between these two great states. The search for advantage and the build-up of enormous arsenals of nuclear weapons resulted in a policy that earned the name of mutually assured destruction. By the 1970s, the credibility of this strategy was being questioned. Flexible response as a strategy for NATO since 1967 meant a perpetual search for greater flexibility, and this policy itself depended upon explicit and well-informed military comparisons. The need for balance and parity became all the more pronounced. Security was found in matching the adversary. Studies of weapons procurement showed the importance of matching the potential opponent.[16] Both states, therefore, retained their interest in balanced forces, however difficult the task of amassing information and drawing up the balance. Neither side could afford to slip too far behind, whether in the conventional or the nuclear field. But this search for balance which provided some hope for a stable and peaceful world, was affected by other considerations.

The USA and the USSR did not begin their relationship on the basis of parity. The United States had a nuclear monopoly in 1945. There was thus created a fear of being caught and overtaken by a determined opponent, against whom the political forces of the years 1945–47 seemed to be working, in Germany and elsewhere. By 1960, the Soviet Union was capable of matching the power of the United States. The Russians could put more troops into battle, and the rivalry was close in most other respects. For the Soviet Union, parity became a great political prize, an acknowledgement that the superiority of the United States was not beyond challenge by a quite different social system, as they liked to put it. An immense and unstoppable capacity had been demonstrated by the USA during the Second World War; ships, jeeps, guns as well as an unlimited flow of butter and provisions, came from the factories and the prairies. The impact on the USSR as on other states, was without parallel. therefore a formal recognition of military parity held great significance for the Soviet Union. The recognition of a military balance and nuclear parity implied a degree of equivalence in other respects. The fundamental benefit for the Soviet Union was thus ideological, as much as the assurance of international stability. The Soviet Union had clawed its way to the status of 'superpower'.

The measure of equality was not easy to establish. The industrial output of the USA and some aspects of technical innovation, would be hard to match. Safer ground for the Soviet Union was military balance. Recognition of this parity which meant so much, was best obtained through arms negotiations. Although this ideological reason was not the only one, for Soviet leaders this became an apparently important reason. Sensitivity over the principle of parity affected the Soviet position on arms and the military balance, and this was increasingly pronounced during the 1980s when so much political weight was placed upon arms talks by governments and the general public alike. The principle of parity was thus implicit in many of the Soviet proposals made by their negotiators in Geneva, and also in Vienna, at the force reduction talks. The concept of agreed ceilings and 'sub-ceilings' suggested parity because it was a common factor, towards which both sides worked. But serious differences impeded progress towards parity. The precise determination of what to include was a major obstacle to agreement. The definition of different categories of arms was another; in the 1980s, this meant particularly the definition of strategic weapons.

The Soviets accepted that strategic arms in the United States and the USSR had different histories, and these different developments raised questions about what to include in any negotiation. Should the long-established nuclear bomber fleet of the USA be included? Should the US aircraft carriers operating in the Atlantic and the Mediterranean, and equipped with nuclear armed fighter-bombers, also be included? In the 1980s the USSR wished to take the French and British nuclear missiles into account. The Soviet position was made clear by Mr Gromyko, then still Foreign Minister, in an interview on 13 January 1985. 'For the Soviet Union medium-range weapons are also strategic weapons. Medium-range arms are medium only in range but as far as the Soviet Union is concerned, they are strategic in nature and in power. These weapons can reach the territory of the Soviet Union. And our medium-range weapons, the SS-20 missiles, the type of weapons against which the United States inveighs day and night, cannot reach the territory of the USA'. This was the heart of the different view. For the government of the USA, strategic arms remained intercontinental arms. Any move on the part of the government of the United States towards a broader recognition of equivalence had immediate political results. The difference of view on weapons had great significance for the relations between the superpowers and inevitably progress was slow and somewhat remote from the rest of international political intercourse.

A clear argument came from Dr Viktor Israelyan, head of the Soviet delegation at the disarmament conference. The United States had been deliberately seeking to prevent parity. 'We regard as correct the opinion of Prof Stanley Cohen of Princeton University that the inability of the US leadership to accept "political parity" with the USSR as an objective reality was the root cause of the crisis of détente'.[17] Thus, he argued that during the START sessions from June 1982 until December 1983, 'the USA sought to get the USSR placed in an unequal position'. But parity in one respect implied parity in others, and the Soviet Union claimed the right to be judged in international relations by the same criteria as the United States. As Dr Israelyan suggested, political parity was at stake. The argument was a good one for the Soviet Union since the USA had either to acknowledge parity or to reaffirm that the two states were not equal, and that the USA was in effect 'superior'. But the government of the United States also sought some degree of stability through arms control and limitation. Many of the bilateral agreements secured more stable military relations between the USA and USSR, although cynics might point out that the SALT treaties were largely irrelevant because they excluded the most important new weapons and those in research and development. A number of treaties were signed, if few were ever ratified, and they all pointed to parity. The Threshold Test Ban treaty, limiting underground nuclear tests to yields below 150 kilotons, and a treaty banning underground nuclear explosions for peaceful uses, were negotiated in 1974 and 1976 respectively. The treaty limiting anti-ballistic missile systems had been signed in May 1972, and a Soviet–American agreement on the prevention of nuclear war was signed and came into operation on 22 June 1973. Although other states were involved in arms agreements and talks during the same years, the major negotiations were between the United States and the Soviet Union. Never before were so many separate issues discussed just between two states. Clearly a political equivalence existed.

The Soviet Union took a distinct advantage in intermediate range nuclear weapons stationed in Europe in the 1970s, and this enabled the Soviets to keep the principle of parity in front of the United States. Once the SS 20 programme had been seen by the governments of NATO states as a direct threat, some response was required. Under Presidents Carter and Reagan, the United States opted for a double response, a 'twin-track' approach in conjunction with European allies. More defence spending on the development of new missiles and further talks were the result. But further talks had henceforth to be on the basis of some kind of parity with the USSR. The clearest statement was the 'zero option' proposed by President Reagan in 1981,[18] a world-wide renunciation by both superpowers of land-based, longer-range intermediate nuclear systems. The proposal was rejected. By 1986, Mr Gorbachev had put forward other suggestions of equal and balanced reductions of nuclear weapons, a kind of 50:50 proposal. By the middle of the 1980s, the basis of talks was parity. As Dr David Owen rather coyly observed: 'we are dealing almost entirely with a political not a military question'.[19] Arms control negotiations opened a path towards other issues and in this lay the heart of the new relationship between the United States and the Soviet Union. What did parity actually mean?

No dishonour fell on the USA in seeking military parity with the USSR. In fact the two possessed approximately equal military power; newspapers and journals were filled with comparative charts and tables which demonstrated this. Less frequently stated were other aspects of Soviet strength, suggesting a capacity to produce and supply war material on a scale comparable to the USA. Strategic surveys of all kinds showed the immense industrial support for the Soviet military.

Perhaps as many as 3000 battle tanks and 1300 fighter aircraft were produced annually. 'Russia is a rich land'; within the frontiers of the Soviet Union were the world's largest deposits of natural gas and the second largest of oil. The USSR produced more steel, cement, cotton, artificial fabrics and railway locomotives than any other state.[20] The Soviet Union was overwhelmingly the largest manufacturer of the world's most destructive weapon, the automatic rifle and pistol. The Kalachnikov was manufactured not only in the USSR, but also under licence in many of the states of the Middle East, in Yugoslavia and China. The Soviet government had the world's second largest navy and the largest fleets of fishing and merchant shipping. In the 1980s the Soviet Union was a truly formidable power. But parity was not only concerned with material things, it concerned political and moral principles.

Political principle had once been the central issue of the Cold War. That principle had been about freedom, and in 1947, for example, the United States was widely regarded as the guardian of political freedom. Its government made the claim and people in many states believed it. The nearer an approach was made to the dividing-line between East and West, in Europe perhaps, or in Berlin itself, the more credible the claim was, and rightly so. A difference clearly existed between the Soviet Union and the United States during the Cold War. However powerful the USSR claimed to be, a substantial distinction remained, the commitment to political freedom. Sir Winston Churchill knew this better than most. For him, power was secondary. The nature of political institutions and the values to which they gave birth distinguished states from one another. Only a change in the political structure altered the political reality and thus might bring a state like the USSR closer to the democratic view of freedom and of appropriate behaviour in international relations. His judgement was severe on the Soviet–German pact of 23 August 1939, the Ribbentrop–Molotov Pact: 'only totalitarian despotism in both countries could have faced the odium of such an unnatural act'.[21] His mistrust of Soviet institutions remained, and therefore also of the bases of Soviet policy. But it became more difficult to sustain the association of the United States with freedom as the earliest years of the Cold War faded in the memory. As with many an attractive but slightly vulgar woman, it was hard to tell exactly when, where and with whom the United States had lost its virginity. For the understanding of Soviet–American relations in the 1980s, the essential point was that it had gone, probably by the time of the Tet offensive in Vietnam in 1968. The way was then clearer for political and moral parity to develop between the superpowers.

When the process of détente began, the United States risked the destruction of a principle in international relations. The acceptance of parity with the Soviet Union was to mean more than just a numerical exercise. Détente had changed the nature of Soviet–American relations in such a way that there could be no renewed Cold War in the 1980s. In the first place, the equation of the United States with freedom as an organising principle in international relations no longer carried the former conviction. Vietnam or the Bay of Pigs could not be forgotten, and they were presented all too easily as a mockery of the grand principle of freedom. The ideal was not easily attained. A belief in freely elected government by a system of plural democracy, in which a properly constituted political opposition could function and where the whole could be scrutinised by a sharp and critical press, was not readily translated into practice. Indeed it was incredibly difficult to establish. But it had looked as if this was the principle for which the United States and the West stood in the Cold War. The governments of the NATO states in the 1980s might see real distinctions between Soviet and western principles in international relations, but this message was not easy to convey.

In the second place, the Soviet Union had been offered an attractive prize, political equivalence with the USA, recognition as a superpower of which there were only two. This had been positively achieved through arms control and the reduction of nuclear arsenals. These negotiations were continued through the years 1972–86. In November President Reagan and Mr Gorbachev delivered a somewhat schoolmasterly rap to their negotiators; 'best efforts' were required to reach a mutually acceptable agreement. The basis was a reaffirmation of Soviet equality. Arms agreements had to mean some degree of equivalence and balance. The greater the pressure by groups calling for nuclear disarmament in Europe, the harder it became for the government of the United States to make a substantial distinction between East and West. In matters nuclear, the only valid distinction was that of numbers, whether of missiles, warheads or explosive capacity. How was the correlation of the United States and freedom to be restored, if at all?

Soviet entanglements afforded some opportunity of re-emphasising the moral and political differences. The argument was clear and President Reagan stated it at a press conference as early as 29 January 1981, days after taking office. In reply to a question about Soviet aims, he said 'so far détente's been a one-way street that the Soviet Union has used to pursue its own aims'.[22] A few plums appeared to fall into the lap of the American administration. The Soviet Union invaded Afghanistan and was caught up in a long war there. A threat of Soviet involvement in the government of Poland existed, against the growing strength and activity of the union, Solidarity. While no actual Soviet military action occurred, the criticism remained at the level of innuendo. In Afghanistan things moved differently. The Soviet support for the communist government in Kaboul involved more than 90,000 troops by December 1981, defending major cities and the arteries of communication. The remoter rural and mountainous areas, especially near the frontier with Pakistan, were not retaken. Several Soviet and Afghan government military thrusts during 1981–85 consolidated the position, but all this enabled President Reagan to raise the principle of freedom. 'The United States will support the cause of a free Afghanistan', he declared in an official statement of 27 December 1981.[23] Once again the issue between the superpowers was freedom; this was not easy to sustain.

President Reagan might have made much of the apparent Soviet determination to extend their influence in parts of the African continent. However, the administration appeared to prefer the firmer ground of Poland and Afghanistan to illustrate Soviet violation of freedom, and the contrast with the position adopted by the United States. The presence of Soviet troops was the vital point. Soviet advisers, technicians and other specialists were present in several African states before

President Reagan took office. Soviet influence was strong in Ethiopia and enmeshed in the fighting there, and in Somalia. They were traced in Angola and other states in southern Africa. The Cubans, close allies of the USSR and largely dependent for material and supply on the Soviet Union, had landed troops and used them both in the Horn of Africa and in Angola. They remained there during the 1980s. But the issues were confused and the precise details difficult to elucidate. Moreover there were too many easy parallels to be made with earlier acts by American governments. Rumours of the involvement of the Central Intelligence Agency in southern Africa were current during the later 1970s, and the United States had certainly assisted the French intervention in the Shaba province of Zaire in 1978. Although Congress had tried to stop such operations, particularly in 1975 and 1976, the government of the United States needed a surer ground on which to develop the theme of fundamental differences between the USA and the Soviet Union. They found such an issue in the question of human rights.

This was not new. Dr Kissinger and President Carter had talked of emphasis on improving the respect of many states for human rights. As international tensions declined world-wide, so the issue of human rights might be linked to détente. In 1975 they were explicitly raised at the Helsinki conference under 'basket three', a series of measures dealing with such humanitarian questions. In the subsequent conferences at Belgrade and Madrid, the representatives of the United States and other West European states pressed for the inclusion of human rights infringements. They were disappointed in the final document at the Belgrade conference which paid only brief attention to the question. At Madrid, the complaints against the Soviet Union for violation of the 'basket three' principles were many, and they were specific. However these meetings considered only cases arising in Europe. President Carter had tried to advance on two fronts in the years 1976–80. He condemned Soviet violations of human rights, and he sought to disassociate the United States from regimes which were known to have a poor record. The policy was consistent and sound, and its intention clear. The USA could not afford to accept parity with the Soviet Union without reservation. The question of human rights was the issue which distinguished the USA and USSR, and which might have restored the association of the United States with the principle of freedom in international politics. His successor continued the pressure on the issue of human rights. They shared the policy of seeking negotiations with the Soviet Union and simultaneously stressing the role of the United States as a state concerned with freedom.

The aim was not easily realised. The USA tied arms control to the wider issue, and here lay the challenge for the Soviet Union in the 1980s. To critics of the Reagan administration, the words of President Reagan and his senior officials looked more like bluff and rhetoric than a genuine concern with moral principles. Their significance was deeper. The President outlined his position on arms control in announcing his determination to proceed with the Strategic Arms Limitation Talks, in November 1981. His speech continued by stressing the principles of his policy: 'Terms like "peace" and "security", we have to say, have little meaning for the oppressed and the destitute. They also mean little to the individual whose state has stripped him of human freedom and dignity . . . We must recognise that progress and the pursuit of liberty is a necessary complement to military security. Nowhere has this fundamental truth been more boldly and clearly stated than in the Helsinki Accords of 1975. These Accords have not yet been translated into living reality'.[24] Four years later, in November 1985, the President, then in his second term, went to Geneva to meet Mr Gorbachev. He pushed forward the same policy of principle and negotiation. He wished to discuss arms control, regional problems and human rights. But there were difficulties in sustaining the momentum over such diverse issues. The interest of the world was on arms control and future negotiations. The principal interest of the Soviet Union was also in this area, where the demonstration of Soviet parity with the United States could most easily be achieved. It was a triumph for the Soviet Secretary General to have limited references to human rights to a short paragraph in the final communiqué for the press, expressing a desire for further communication between the two peoples. The demands for more specific consideration of liberties and infringements of human rights were not met.

However some of the difficulty was of American making. It was still not clear that the United States government chose its allies and its 'friends' with the principles of freedom and respect for the individual in mind. During the 1980s the burden of the past continued to weigh down the government in Washington. They were unable to rid themselves of the memories of past regimes that had earned American support, particularly that of South Vietnam. By 1986, a break had been made with 'Baby Doc' Duvalier, of Haiti, who fled to France in February; and later in the same month, with President Marcos of the Philippines, an ally of the United States for twenty years. But the contradiction between policies and principles, or rhetoric as the critics of the USA preferred, was sharpest in Central America.

By 1985 the government of the United States was accused of aiding terrorism in the whole region. The CIA was alleged to have supported disruption and lawlessness. Military supplies and training had been offered to ill-disciplined forces, fighting legitimate governments. Corrupt governments were kept in office with United States connivance. At the Budapest meeting of the European Security and Cooperation Conference in November 1985, the Soviet delegation accused the United States of genocide, racism, anti-Semitism and censorship.[25] Although the session was concerned with Europe, the attack had events in El Salvador and Nicaragua in mind—hence the surprise of the American delegates and others. With greater logic, the Nicaraguan government withdrew its Ambassador to Washington. In the autumn of 1985, the US government was on trial at the International Court of the Hague for human rights infringements in Central America. This case provoked the government into a decision not to accept the jurisdiction of the Court automatically.

The difficulty was not new; decades of embroilment in Central America, seen in the files of US governments, and revealed publicly by invasion and less open political involvement, lay behind the events of the 1980s. President Carter had already grappled with the oppressive regime of Anastasio Somoza, being reluctant to provide arms and insisting on respect for humanitarian values, if not always successfully. The government of the United States finally abandoned him in 1979.

The victory of the Sandinista movement which the removal of Somoza regime ensured, brought two significant results. First, Nicaragua acquired a government with an organised Marxist ideology—organised in so far as there were party and institutions leaning in that direction. Moreover, they set an example for other states in the region. The second result was that Soviet and Cuban influence was likely to increase on the Central American isthmus. In the next five years, the Sandinistas received aid from both, in particular military aid to replace the support which President Carter had given them but which had subsequently been stopped. By the time that the new Republican administration had taken office in 1981, Nicaragua was clearly aligned with the Cubans, and was supporting insurrection in neighbouring states, including El Salvador. This was the view of the government of the United States and created a dilemma for the President. The nature and extent of Nicaraguan support for revolutionary movements in Central America was not clear. At the very least the success of the Sandinistas was an encouragment to others fighting in neighbouring states. On the other hand United States' support for existing regimes which were not communist would invite criticism and opposition. There was persistent evidence of arbitrary and sometime brutal repression of opposition. Yet to do nothing was to invite the success of movements allied with Cuba and ultimately with the Soviet Union. Moreover there was little confidence that these 'progressive' movements would guarantee respect for human rights. They were no less likely to escape condemnation for violation of rights than the regimes that they replaced and the dictatorships of old. In Nicaragua the Creole people of the Atlantic coast voiced continual complaints against the Sandinista government after the change of regime in 1979. Central America therefore became a crucial test for the principles of US foreign policy.

The basis of that policy was support for those regimes that offered some prospect of plural democracy, some political stability and sufficient openness to allow for the respect for human rights. Where this was adequate, the United States would offer aid. This was both military, for the fight against revolutionary movements, and social and economic. The link between aid and performance was an updated version of the linking of aid to democracy of the Kennedy era, the so-called 'Alliance for Progress' of 1961. Congress urged greater respect for law as well as for humanitarian policies. In 1984 and 1985 the Secretary of State, Mr George Schultz, was more and more outspoken on the need for unambiguous respect for these values. Governments had to make their humanitarian policies clear. He pursued this case in Honduras and El Salvador. In the latter case the political future became more fragile. Revolutionary activity increased after the Sandinista success, and military aid was resumed already before the change of administration in Washington in January 1981. The position was aggravated by the assassination of Archbishop Romero in March 1980 and the public outcry in the USA after three American nuns were assassinated in December 1980. Such acts were committed by both the insurgents and the security forces, thus making the task of the new administration more difficult. However, the election of the centre-right government of Jose Napoleon Duarte in El Salvador confirmed the judgement of the President that in this regime lay the best prospect of democracy and reform as well as justice.

But the policy was full of snares. The elections in Nicaragua in 1984 were denounced by the Reagan administration as corrupt, in contrast to those held earlier in El Salvador, a distinction not so clear to all observers. Further opposition was encouraged in Nicaragua, and the support given to the anti-Sandinista campaign by the USA in 1982 was continued throughout the next years. The parties, clustered around the label FDN, a Nicaraguan democratic force, had a military organisation, the Contras. However, the human rights question did not disappear. Many of the Contra troops were recruited among the National Guard, the repressive units of the former dictator, Somoza. Their humanitarian record led Congress to insist on removing all military aid from the United States. In 1985 an aid budget for the opposition in Nicaragua was voted—$27 million for non-military purposes. Fears of direct involvement were groundless in the years 1981–86, apart from rumours of CIA operations, including the mining of harbours in 1984. Yet many of the close allies of the USA adopted a policy more sympathetic to the Sandinista government than that of President Reagan. They were also more critical of the regime in El Salvador. Trade agreements were signed between the Sandinista government and Spain, Belgium and Sweden. Nicaraguan cotton was the subject of a trade agreement with Japan, and the Canadians purchased meat as well as permitting the opening of a trade delegation in Toronto. Other trade deals were arranged with East European states, especially for the purchase of Nicaraguan bananas.[26] The French government incurred American displeasure in 1981 and 1982 when they sold military equipment to the government in Managua, including helicopters and small arms.

The dilemma that faced the government of the United States had a familiar aspect. Mixed support from the closest allies blended with allies in the region of doubtful value and quality, as well as an opponent whose political success encouraged other revolutionary movements. There was a superficial resemblance to the case of Cuba and the Castro regime in 1959 and 1960. But the position was quite different and more difficult. Cuba could be isolated, but Nicaragua lay on the isthmus, adjacent to El Salvador, Costa Rica and Honduras, with frontiers hard to control. The Nicaraguan regime was openly Marxist and had close links with the Soviet Union, whereas Cuba only moved in that direction after the fall of the Batista regime in 1959. Moreover Cuba was effectively isolated physically after the missiles crisis of 1962. In the 1980s the government of the United States could not easily reconcile strategic objectives and the isolation of the Nicaraguan regime and a concern for human rights and freedom. There had been strong arguments for insisting on sympathetic and stable regimes in the Caribbean and Central America in the past. The more forceful applications of the Monroe Doctrine in the nineteenth and twentieth centuries had occurred there. The area was critical for the sea lanes of the Gulf of Mexico and for the Pacific coast, although the importance to the USA had declined. Their influence in the Panama Canal Zone had gone with the Treaty of 1978 which passed sovereignty to the government of Panama. But in the 1980s the argument for a strategic intervention was complicated by the international relationship between the USA and the USSR. The principle of a secure zone of influence in which only sympathetic governments were acceptable was the argument applied by the

Soviet Union to Eastern Europe. It was precisely this view that permitted communist regimes to appear and continue in that part of Europe closest to the Soviet Union. For President Reagan to use the same argument was to encourage the view that identical criteria were applicable in international politics to both the USA and the USSR. The result was the shuffling policy of the years 1980–86, hoping to limit the success of revolutionary regimes and to continue the demand for respect for human rights.

President Reagan grasped this difficult nettle at the start of his first term of office. He was quite definite about his policy for the entire region. On 18 November 1981, he reviewed his recent discussions with President Herrera Campins of Venezuela. They had 'discussed what can be done to promote peace, freedom, and representative government in that part of the world'.[27] The government of the United States supported the attempts of the Contadora states (Venezuela, Colombia, Mexico and Panama) to bring an end to the war in Central America. Also in 1983, the United States was involved in the politics of the island of Grenada, apparently in direct contradiction to the proclaimed principles of independence. But the case was *sui generis,* quite different from other events whatever the suggestions that this was a major infringement of principles in international relations.

When troops from the USA invaded the Caribbean island in October 1983, they came to crush a Cuban-backed administration that had been implicated in the overthrow of the previous regime, also of the political left, and not a right-wing military dictatorship, of Mr Bishop. Mr Bishop had been assassinated. The operation was rapid, involved no long term commitment by the United States, and had the support of other governments in the Caribbean, including member governments of the British Commonwealth. The principle in the name of which the operation had taken place was the defence of free institutions against arbitrary and undemocratic manipulation. The difficulty was to argue this with conviction outside the region.

For the Soviet Union, the American involvement in Central America and the Caribbean basin held no threat. If bipolarity was the basis of world order, this division into spheres of interest had long been acceptable. The position for the government of the United States was more difficult, and the drift of policy remained equivocal. The presidency of Mr Reagan had a formidable record in many respects; there had been no extended military involvement or disgrace, he had continued the rearmament programme commenced by President Carter, and, with unemployment down and the economy sounder than critics had predicted, he was smoothly re-elected in 1984. Communism had not encroached on the world that he regarded as 'free'. However, the need to distinguish clearly between the democratic United States and the totalitarian Soviet Union remained. The pressure for parity and the emphasis on nuclear arms and their control and limitation, did nothing to expose the differences that existed between them. In March 1983, the President made a speech referring to the development of a new space defence programme, expensive, complicated and requiring several years of development, but intended to make nuclear weapons of the 1980s obsolete, and the world a safer place. This strategic defence initiative, as the programme came to be called, had important implications for the political relations between the USA and the USSR. In some respects the programme began to assume a very major position in their relations during 1985 and 1986. The military and technical feasibility were closely linked to the politics of SDI, but were nevertheless tangential to the international relationship between the two superpowers.

The President of the United States made a strong commitment to his space defence programme. By the end of 1985, $26 billion had been earmarked for research, and many universities were participating in the work on electronics, concentrated energy sources and lasers. By the same time the positive commitment was so great that abandonment would have amounted to personal defeat for Mr Reagan; the programme was no mere bargain chip, to be dropped in return for Soviet concessions. The technical difficulties were secondary to the political implications, as were the immediate military consequences for NATO strategy. Some argued that the strategy of retaliation, of mutual assured destruction, was outmoded and lacked credibility. Perhaps it was even immoral in its implications, and a defence against ballistic missiles in space, based on layers of defence systems, such as the SDI, might allow a surer and more credible strategy. But these arguments for and against, in common with the mixed reception that the programme received among the European allies of the United States, did not go to the root of the politics of SDI.

There was no total agreement in Washington in 1985 about the implications of the programme for the USSR. However there was agreement that it would be serious. Some applauded the fact that the need to match the research would strain Soviet resources of all kinds. This was the argument of the more 'hawkish' spirits in Washington. Others, including the Secretary of State, Mr Schultz, feared the consequences of thus pushing the Soviet economy and resources to the limit in striving to cover the work on lasers, kinetic energy and the many tracking and surveillance systems which the programme required. It was true that President Reagan had suggested the sharing of the technology with the USSR, partly relieving the Soviet economy of the severest strains. Such a proposal avoided a Soviet pre-emptive strike, preventing the development of the programme, or the build-up of such arsenals of weapons that the new programme might be 'saturated' and therefore inoperative. These arguments edged towards the central political factor. The strategic defence initiative marked out the United States from the USSR in international relations. Such a possible development of space defence was so significantly different that the primacy of the USA was reasserted, and equality between the two states could scarcely be seriously maintained. The President of the USA was even in the position of 'offering' a share in the successful programme to the Soviet Union. Soviet reactions indicated that the programme was taken most seriously. Mr Gorbachev spoke out against the scheme, before the meeting at Geneva in November 1985, and at the meeting, and after the meeting. A Soviet view of the programme was precisely that it was 'part of a general offensive plan intended for upsetting the strategic parity, gaining military superiority'.[28] Indeed it had that effect and thus afforded the opportunity to argue that there were other, deeper differences between the two states.

By 1985 it was not clear that enough had been done to restore the credibility of the United States as the upholder of the principle of freedom in international politics. Mr Schultz hinted at the importance of human rights in United States foreign policy, as he did in December 1985, on an official visit to Bucharest. His government could not always manage to link strategic preferences and military advantage to the ideological demand for respect for human rights and freedom in politics. President Reagan's assertion that 'the pursuit of liberty is a necessary complement to military security' was a distinct contrast to the remarks of the Soviet foreign secretary, Mr Shevadnadze. At a meeting commemorating the tenth anniversary of the Helsinki meeting, he declared, 'it is necessary to separate carefully ideological disagreements and inter-state relations'. A vast distance of principle continued to exist between the USA and the Soviet Union in 1985.

The 1980s were therefore no simple continuation of détente. The gap between the two great federal states had lost some of the sense of identity of purpose which characterised the era of President Nixon and Dr Kissinger. The emphasis was then on shared functions in international relations. Only in arms control and negotiations has this emphasis remained strong. But there came no certainty that the United States had regained a moral edge which had been keenest when their troops moved across Europe in 1944 and 1945. Perhaps only at the border between East and West Berlin was the difference between the states self-evidently a matter of principle still in 1985. But that border was an anachronism, frozen in an institutional form of 1945, marginally modified by the four-power agreement of 1971 and the wall, built in 1961.

A paradox of the years of détente was that the anticipated linkage between arms control and other political disputes had not occurred. It was difficult to move from arms negotiations to the discussion of 'regional' problems at the Geneva summit of November 1985. Linkage may have become an illusion, like the convergence of the two superpowers. In the 1980s bipolarity did not mean the division of the world into spheres of interest. Soviet and American influence suffered major modifications, not least among their allies and the division of the world into the two camps was threatened and, some might argue, had disappeared in the age of Reagan and Gorbachev. In so far as this was so, the disengagement of military balance and hence parity in that sense, from the overall political relations which included spheres in interest, was a principal cause. The test of this change for the two superpowers came in their relations with their own allies.

NOTES

1. N. Chomsky *et al., Superpowers in Collision* (London, 1982), p. 10.
2. The Rt Hon Dr David Owen MP, lecturing to the Royal United Services Institute, 19 October 1983.
3. S.E. Ambrose, *Rise to Globalism* (London, 1983), p. 417.
4. The United States supplied arms and trained its forces with the Egyptians throughout the 1980s.
5. Dr V. Israelyan, head of the Soviet delegation at the European conference on disarmament, 'The arms race—who is to blame'?, *NATO's Sixteen Nations,* December 1984–January 1985, p. 19.
6. *Recalling the past for the sake of the future* (Moscow, 1985; in translation), p. 130.
7. In an interview with Walter Cronkite, CBS News, 3 March 1981, *Public Papers of the Presidents of the United States: Ronald Reagan* (Washington, 1982).
8. *Strategic Survey 1984* (London), p. 36. This curious judgement was made without reference to the tensions during the Vietnam War, the 1968 crisis in Czechoslovakia, and perhaps even the Cuban missile crisis.
9. Linda Miller, 'The foreign policy of Reagan II', *American Foreign policy,* April 1985, p. 72.
10. J. Kastl, 'The CSCE review meeting in Madrid', *NATO Review* 1983, no. 5, p. 15.
11. A full discussion is provided by Nicole Gnesotto, 'Conference on disarmament in Europe opens in Stockholm', *NATO Review,* 1983, no. 6, p. 1 ff. The measure considered included exchange of information on disposition and command of forces, prior notification of military activities and observation and verification procedures.
12. See the discussion in Ambrose, *op. cit.,* pp. 394-6.
13. Communiqué of the special meeting of NATO Foreign and Defence Ministers, Brussels, 12 December 1979.
14. The Federal Minister of Defence, *White Paper,* 1983 (translation published by the Defence Ministry), p. 196.
15. *Ibid.,* p. 241.
16. See Mary Kaldor, *European Defence Industries* (Sussex, 1972).
17. Israelyan, *Loc. cit.,* p. 19.

18. The 'zero/zero' solution for Soviet and American land-based intermediate range systems was proposed on 18 November 1981, and formed the basis of the draft treaty proposed by the United States' negotiator at the Geneva conference, Ambassador Nitze, on 2 February 1982.
19. *Loc. cit.*
20. A vivid account of Soviet economic resources was provided by the West German periodical *Der Spiegel,* no. 4, January 1982, p. 86.
21. Winston Churchill, *The Second World War* (London, 1949), vol. 1, p. 351.
22. President's news conference, 29 January 1981, *Public Papers,* p. 57.
23. Statement on the situation in Afghanistan, 27 December 1981, *Public Papers,* p. 1199-200.
24. 'Remarks to members of the National Press Club on arms reduction and nuclear weapons', 18 November 1981, *Public Papers,* p. 1067.
25. This was reported in *Le Monde,* 27 November 1985.
26. Press report, fully presented in *Le Monde,* 31 October 1985.
27. *Public Papers,* p. 1067.
28. *Recalling the Past for the Sake of the Future,* p. 130. See also McGeorge Bundy, George F. Kennan, Robert McNamara and Gerard Smith, 'The President's choice: star wars or arms control', *Foreign Affairs,* 1984, pp. 264-78.

2 The Allies

The strength of alliances was directly dependent upon the tensions of the Cold War. This grim feature had characterised the progress of the alliances on both sides of the capitalist/communist divide since 1945. It had also controlled the pace of integration in Western Europe and the convergence between the blocs of states. The major steps in the development of alliances and in the march towards European integration coincided with the tenser moments of East–West relations. This has been well established and documented.[1] 1948 brought both the Brussels Treaty and the Berlin blockade after the deterioration in East–West political cooperation in the German zones. The following year saw the first moves in the West, creating the North Atlantic Treaty Organisation. 1950 was a year of spreading Cold War tensions, but also brought France and West Germany together in the European Coal and Steel Communities. The outbreak of the Korean War completed and confirmed the universality of the Cold War. No state or continent could escape the implications. The Soviet invasion of Hungary in 1956 concentrated the minds of those West European leaders who were discussing the process of integration. The creation of a common market was the result. Eventually the effect of détente was to remove the pressure for integrated policies. In the East the experience was similar. The Warsaw Pact was created in response to the rearming of West Germany within NATO. But in the 1980s new experiences muddled the apparently and deceptively straightforward analysis of international relations since 1945.

In many ways the Cold War simplified international

relations. President Roosevelt promised that US troops would leave European soil within two years of the end of war. Forty years later there were still almost 350,000 in Europe. Thousands of others from the US navy and airforce were involved in the defence of the Atlantic seaways and the western airspace from the North polar regions to the Tropic of Cancer. Joseph Stalin had made no extravagant promises in 1945. In 1985 there were also Soviet soldiers and airmen stationed in many of the quarters that they had occupied in 1945. Indeed since 1948 they had come further West, into Czechoslovakia. The military agreement which had come into existence in 1955 in Eastern Europe, the Warsaw Pact, celebrated its thirtieth anniversary intact, except for Albania. Occasional suggestions that the Romanian government might change its policy never materialised. Europe, in short, has had a consistent military history since 1945, divided into two very heavily armed alliances. The few remaining neutral and non-aligned states have been left to fend for themselves.

The antagonism had created the status of 'superpower'. The test of this coveted but awesome responsibility has been the ability to attract allies. Neither the People's Republic of China nor France found their governments tied into alliances and treaty obligations in the same way as the USA and the Soviet Union, despite possessing nuclear weapons. But by 1980 the Cold War had thawed, and détente had loosened the bonds which restricted foreign policy. Some of the formal alliance structures of the Cold War outside Europe had vanished with changes of regime, of policy and with the modification of United States commitments. Thus the South-East Asian Treaty Organisation disappeared, leaving a weakened pact between the governments of the USA, Australia and New Zealand. The Central Treaty Organisation collapsed after the overthrow of the Shah's rule in Iran, although the military effectiveness of this treaty had long been doubted. Political and military confidence had been undermined by the Turkish invasion of Cyprus in 1974 and by the British policy of withdrawal from east of Suez after 1956.

A more cautious approach characterised the policy of the government of the USSR. In the military and political obligations of the Soviet Union, there were fewer long-term agreements. The principle remained that of bilateralism. No overarching arrangement encompassed Soviet diplomatic ties. Some of the treaties were stable and apparently successful. In the Middle East, the bilateral bond between Syria and the USSR remained firm into the 1980s. On the other hand, more caution had been exercised after the experience of rejection, when links with the USSR were cut by the Egyptian government in 1976. The need for such careful building of contacts was demonstrated in January 1986 when the Marxist-Leninist regime of the South Yemen, associated with Moscow since 1969, crumbled in a civil war. Soviet citizens, experts, advisers, trade officials, all emerged from the Aden woodwork, nervous of the outcome after the return in 1985 of Abdel Fatah Ismail from exile in Moscow. This leader established an alternative pro-Soviet faction in the central committee of the Yemeni Communist Party. Thus even in regimes such as this the Soviet links were tenuous. The numbers of close diplomatic ties between the superpowers and other states remained large in 1980, but the interrelationship between the many agreements was not consistent and less clearly permanent. The place of alliances and alliance systems in international relations in the 1980s was altogether more fluid. The relations between the USA and the USSR were therefore affected by this dynamism.

The international framework of the 1950s and 1960s in which the superpowers sat, spider-like in the centre of a web of associated states, has gone. Even in the most extensive and the oldest of alliances, those in Europe, relations among allies had changed by 1980. No erosion of the military agreements in Europe had occurred. The concentrations of troops and armour and the support structures for these armies were all so great that no easy disengagement was possible. However the political presuppositions on which the military organisations were based began to change after détente. The nature and role of the superpower was questioned. There were some exceptions. The Soviet-dominated economic and trading partnership, COMECON, grew in importance. The original European member states were joined by others, including Vietnam and Cuba. After the victory of the Sandinistas in Nicaragua, trading and assistance was extended to that regime which was effectively incorporated into the organisation. But this example of the extension of superpower influence was the exception rather than the rule, and other institutions faced greater political problems.

Political relations within the Warsaw Pact and within NATO were concerned with three aspects of international relations. The first and potentially the most important and disruptive was a convergence between East and West. There was no let-up in this process during the 1980s, although it began many years earlier. The second aspect, to some extent a result of the continuing convergence, was the relationship between the nuclear superpowers and their allies. Different issues divided governments after 1980, although the fact of a divergence of view was not new. The third aspect of international relations was the impact on European integration. Changes in the relations between East and West, and changes in the relations within the alliances, suggested the prospect of greater integration. In West Europe, where the pace of integration was strong, more states joined the European Community—Greece in 1981, Spain and Portugal in 1986. Cold War had pulled governments closer together. After the passing of Cold War and the evolution of détente, the logic of integration was not so certain. All these aspects of European politics worked on the internal politics of alliances.

Convergence has a long history. However the political consequences became sharper in the 1980s. Diplomatic contacts were well-established between the governments of West and East Europe, as they were between these states and the two superpowers. Since the successful achievement of West German *Ostpolitik* in 1970 and 1972, the previously impenetrable frontier had been crossed by the signing of many agreements. The expansion of trade became the striking feature of this convergence during the 1970s. The question was posed for the future, whether this development carried permanent and significant political implications. Some signs were ominous. A division of interest opened between the superpowers and allied states. Although all of the states of Europe and the alliances were involved in the growing interdependence of trade and economies, the European states were more deeply involved than either of the superpowers.

West European states bought and sold in all East European states and in all manner of goods. East European governments all sought to expand their earnings from foreign currencies, preferably dollars and Deutschmarks, but other western money was also acceptable. Western businesses invested in factories and railways, in all aspects of the infrastructure and industry of the East. Some of the contracts were huge and major debts were accrued, amounting to a new degree of interdependence. The largest single project of these years and the most controversial was the building of the pipeline to carry natural gas from the eastern region of the USSR. This required contracts with several companies, from many states, for the building of the valves and pumping stations as well as the pipe runs for the extraction and distribution of gas. By 1980 the contracts were valued at $15 milliards, a sum equivalent to Soviet exports to all European community countries in the same year. But the trade benefited European and not US companies.

The trade and investment was clearly mutually beneficial. A network of credit arrangements and contract brokers had been created. In Western Europe trade of this kind protected at least some jobs during the period of growing unemployment—as many as 1 million according to some journalists in the Federal Republic alone. The complicated and often long-term contracts to build factories had many advantages for such firms as Fiat of Italy, a pioneer in this field, and Rhône-Poulenc, the French chemical producer which was engaged in the building of plant in the Soviet Union. The easy purchase of modern equipment and of a production process which did not take years to research, develop and install, was an important saving for the governments of Eastern Europe. There were other benefits. The innovative skills of capitalist production management could be imported without the costs of experimentation and possibly failure. For the West, the lingering recession which followed the price rise of crude oil in 1973 could be partly offset by such profitable deals.

Poland invested in the most modern western managerial and production techniques to a greater extent than other East European governments. By 1980, the Polish government had installed more automated factory equipment, especially robots, than most western states, very many more than were in use in the United Kingdom.[2] These systems cost a great deal and drained foreign currency holdings and ate into credit arrangements. Subsequent difficulties in payment affected production performance and the provision of spares and replacements as well as the financial position of the Polish government. Even robots proved sensitive to matters of debt. Thus contracts between East and West grew in the newer industrial techniques, in electronics and in micro-electrical goods. The East European states bought heavily in the world of the micro-chip and miniaturisation techniques. The speed of innovation in this area, producing new items at an accelerating rate, placed ever greater pressures on the USSR and its allies and required yet more purchases of goods in these categories. Sluggish domestic responses in markets like information storage and teleprinters, forced the Soviet Union to buy in Japan, the USA and especially in Western Europe. The trade was profitable for the suppliers, if sometimes difficult to organise. The need to find foreign currencies was not always met, and the eastern states turned to a system of barter, offering other commodities in order to complete purchase. An entire brokerage in such deals developed, based principally in London, during the 1970s, enabling western firms to complete contracts, often without receiving cash payment from the communist buyers. What had begun as a simple trading relationship, had become an extremely complicated network of links and commercial enterprise.

Only dire circumstances justified the rupture of these commercial links. In 1980 and 1981, the government of the USA discovered how difficult and how dire the circumstance had to be. In the immediate gloom after the Soviet invasion of Afghanistan, the government of the United States attempted to persuade the NATO allies to stop some of the trade and investment flowing to the USSR. In particular attention focused on the contracts for the natural gas pipeline. The governments of the Federal Republic, United Kingdom and France refused to respond to the request from Washington. They allowed the contracts to be honoured and the many companies involved to continue work. This was partly because of the consequences for exports and employment, partly the decision was influenced by the refusal of the government in Washington to stop the export of grain from the USA to the Soviet Union. What this episode revealed was the extent of the change that had occurred in Europe. The United States stood in a different relationship to the USSR than did European allies. Although there was a peak in East–West trade in the late 1970s, and governments became aware of the implications of too close and intense an interdependence, the level remained fairly constant into the 1980s, and significantly greater than direct Soviet-bloc trade with the USA.

The levels of trading between the USA and communist states in Europe were low. Imports from East bloc states were very low, less than 1 per cent of United States imports through the decade 1970–80.[3] Exports were higher but never constant; they tended to reach monetary peaks. The grain embargo imposed by President Carter cut sharply into this side of trade balance. With the exception of some items of 'modern technology', the trade was also less politically sensitive than that of the Europeans. They became involved in the creation of communication systems, and traded in commodities which helped the overall growth of Eastern economies and their total productive capacity. Moreover, the trade was often in more highly labour-intensive goods than that of the United States; more European jobs were thus at risk. The grain trade which had been the largest element in the American trade, was not a monopoly for the USA. The Argentine and Australia were competitors for the grain market, and the share of the Soviet cereals market held by the United States fell from c.80 per cent before 1981 to 25–30 per cent by 1984.[4] In matters economic, therefore, a divide had opened on the question of trade with the East between the United States and its European allies. Whatever the fears however, it was a major distortion to claim that this was a harmful degree of 'dependence'. The factor of East–West economic interdependence only became important because the government of the USA had attempted to make it of political significance. Even the Federal Republic of Germany did not exceed a level of 6 per cent of its total trade with the state of the Eastern bloc.[5] The continuing convergence of economic interests in Europe was therefore not a major source of inter-allied tension, because it lacked real substance.

Where the trade mattered, governments intervened to safeguard the security of the alliance. This was achieved in those goods which might be used for military purposes by the Soviet Union and its allies. The USA and its NATO partners constantly kept such items under review and, if necessary, prohibited completion of contracts.

Divergence among allies was more serious in its political implications. This was so partly because there were many different issues and degrees of disunity within the two alliances. None of this was particularly new in the 1980s. The novelty came from the freedom with which different policies were pursued. A fresh confidence and release came with the widespread belief that a war in Europe was unlikely. It was perhaps this confidence that encouraged quite startling political developments in Eastern Europe. The government of the Soviet Union faced the prospect of a Polish government under perpetual threat. Social disruption, a workers' organisation and the Roman Catholic Church challenged the government through the 1980s. The government of General Jaruzelski which had followed that of Mr Giereck, attempted to contain the protests against the suppression of liberties and the price, and availability, of bread. The question was therefore posed, how seriously the military pact was affected by these events. There was little to suggest that the great strains in Poland and the imposition of martial law damaged the Warsaw Pact. In many ways the Soviet Union emerged undisturbed by events in Poland. The police and the military, including the civil guard, had not turned against the government. Moreover the calm policy adopted by the Soviet government had apparently been successful. No Soviet troops had been in action on Polish streets. The government in Warsaw had survived by the application of a resolute policy, even if this determination had been shaken by dramatic clashes with their opponents. The government withstood the defiance of union leaders like Lech Walesa. Even the assassination of the Roman Catholic priest, Father Popielushko by over-zealous security men in 1984 failed to bring down more than abuse on the government. The priest had been a popular and outspoken supporter of Solidarity and his death brought public and defiant demonstrations, but a year after the trial of his assassins, Poland was still governed by the Jaruzelski regime. Martial law had been lifted, and the General himself had become President and less immediately concerned with day-to-day events. The ending of martial law was a triumph for Soviet policy. The grip of the USSR had emerged without the kind of action that had been thought necessary in East Germany and Poland in 1953, in Hungary in 1956 and, less violently, in Czechoslovakia in 1968.

However the politicians in the Kremlin simultaneously observed a Hungarian government in the midst of a major programme of liberalisation. There was some irony in this. The economic transformation was taking place under the authority of Mr Kadar who had been appointed in 1956, as a direct result of the intervention of the Soviet forces which crushed the October rising and the so-called Hungarian revolution. By 1985, a measured programme of economic change had been implemented. This brought more consumer choice, new standards of competition and above all considerable exchange with the West European states. However the programme remained an economic policy and did not include wider social and political aspects as had been the case in 1956. Also the process had been slow and allowed time for adjustment both inside Hungary and by the USSR. Nevertheless the consequences for the socialist closed economic systems were incalculable in the 1980s. This was convergence of economic doctrines of a different order from growth in East–West trade. But the evolution of the Hungarian economy in the 1980s was also a demonstration that economies once regarded as narrow and inflexible were able to adapt. Dissent among the peoples of the Eastern European states and variations in government policies were rather successfully handled by the Soviet Union in the years 1980–86. Their troops remained in their barracks and the influence of Moscow, carefully registered by western journalists, was tolerantly and subtly applied. Soviet authority was certainly present, as the cancellation of visits by East European leaders to the Federal Republic in 1984 illustrated. The USSR emerged from the events of the 1980s in Poland and Hungary as from those in other East European partners in the Warsaw Pact, without serious undermining of its authority.

The government of the United States also faced differences

of view with European allies. Some of these differences concerned strictly East–West politics. Such was the request from Washington that the European governments support action against the Soviet Union after the invasion of Afghanistan. The possibility of Soviet direct involvement in the internal affairs of Poland in 1980–83 was linked by the United States government to the need for more than public denunciations. Few West European states cooperated. Most confined the response to formal statements expressing disapproval. There were many examples of Soviet action or inaction which invited such denunciations. The failure to release dissidents and Jews who wished to emigrate to Israel. All of these brought more or less concerted protests from the government of the United States and from major allies, particularly the United Kingdom, France and the Federal Republic of Germany. Sustained pressure on Solidarity in Poland was greeted with similar disapproval. By 1986 this particular issue had faded from the scene and was no longer a focal point of East–West tension. President Mitterrand, hitherto a severe critic of the Polish government, even met General Jaruzelski in Paris—much to the irritation of some of the French leader's supporters. However the range of possible action that NATO states were considering in order to bring pressure upon the government of the Soviet Union and to make public the nature of the Soviet state and political system, was to be broadened. Economic sanctions were what the American administration would have preferred.

Such a policy appeared to have many attractions. There was plenty of scope for flexibility, what commodities were included? Exactly which Eastern states would be involved? Would existing agreements be excluded? What of future investments and contracts? Such a degree of flexibility might be attained, that economic sanctions might be used as subject matter for negotiation and bargaining; good behaviour brought rewards. The appeal of this diplomacy was consistent with other United States requirements. Congress liked sanctions since there was no risk of military involvement. Costs were not crippling to the USA and there was a good margin for negotiation. But the governments of the West European allies were less impressed during the 1980s when the government of the United States requested economic sanctions not only against the USSR but also against Libya, early in 1986, and their consideration against the Republic of South Africa. The riots, police controls and instability in South Africa from 1984 brought varied reaction from the NATO states. The government of France applied a form of sanction prohibiting new investments. The other governments were more cautious. In the case of Libya, there was no response to the request for sanctions made by the government of the USA in an effort to apply some pressure on the Libyan government and force a reconsideration of support for terrorists. Trade advantages went far to explain this reluctance; the total value of United States–Libyan trade in 1984 was $210 million, and that of France was $1020 million. The Italians had by far the largest trade, valued at $4400 million.[6] Such different interests also affected the European responses to appeals for economic sanctions against the Soviet Union. The value of United States trade with the Soviet Union in 1981 was $2713 million, and had dropped slightly by 1983, to $2375 million. This was not only a tiny part of the total trade value of the USA, but much smaller than the value of, for example, the trade between the Federal Republic and the USSR; worth $7332 million in 1981, this had risen to $8862 by 1983. Moreover, the larger portion of United States trade was export, predominantly cereals, unlike the varied commerce of European states. Consequently economic sanctions did not work. The West European states did not follow the lead, or hints, given by the government in Washington: East–West trade in Europe survived, demonstrating the different priorities.

However no permanent bitterness was created between the USA and the West European allies. If the pipeline and other contracts were not broken, a general agreement was expressed on the need to be aware of too strong a dependence upon East European investment and commerce. In particular there was a sharpened sensitivity to goods with military application. Closer scrutiny by governments in the West was directed towards the trade in electronic goods, in particular those relating to computers and similar equipment. Economics was not the test of inter-allied cooperation. Indeed the structure of NATO was intact, strengthened by the inclusion of Spain in

1982. Despite intimations of withdrawal, the Greek government remained a member of the alliance, the withdrawal symptoms overcome by practical defence requirements in the face of growing Soviet naval forces in the eastern Mediterranean and the solidly pro-Soviet regimes of nearby Bulgaria and Romania. The planned deployment of nuclear weapons had occurred, although there was some delay in obtaining the approval of the governments and the representative assemblies of the Netherlands and Belgium. The NATO governments had learned in the 1960s that there were nuances in their many views of the Soviet Union and their assessments of the Soviet threat. Governments in the United States had seemingly always understood the fact of this difference since the origins of the Cold War, and the contemporary differences were soon accommodated and were not permitted to build up a serious division within the alliance.

This was not true of all political issues in the 1980s however. European peoples and governments looked askance at suggestions of a new emphasis in the foreign policy of the United States. There was a fear that Europe was no longer the major priority. The provision of new missiles was a gauge of American intentions, but other aspects of US policies were less reassuring. The new dimensions of mobility and flexibility by US armed forces already suggested new commitments and priorities. The rapid deployment force was an extra-European force in composition and location, especially appropriate for operations in the Middle East or the Americas. The United States navy had received substantial increases in funds and had become a force of some 600 vessels in the mid-1980s. Such indications of new priorities went further than the traditional differences of view taken on both sides of the Atlantic. The latent tensions between the USA and European allies threatened to emerge more strongly. Identity of view on European matters did not mean an identical view on all aspects of international relations.

The hidden conflict of view and even of interests had been revealed at the time of the involvement of the USA in the war in Vietnam. European criticism had been sharp and no government gave active support. The more strongly interventionist policy of the Reagan administration in Central

America also brought criticism in West Europe. The degree of disapproval expressed by governments varied a great deal. The most direct opposition came from the French government. This was particularly directed towards the conflict in Nicaragua between the Sandinista government and their opponents. In 1981 and 1982, President Mitterrand approved limited arms sales to the Nicaraguan government, and a visit by the then Defence Minister, Charles Hernu, to Washington revealed the gap between the two views. However no lasting damage was done to Franco-American relations. The matter was significant in the different emphasis in policy; France, whether Gaullist or Socialist, preferred a less committed foreign policy and clung to the principle of support for what the government regarded as a legitimate sovereignty. The American operation on the island of Grenada, although a minor affair, caused public resentment in the United Kingdom for the manner in which British interests and views were ignored. Local Commonwealth support for the United States was more important for the government in Washington. But the episode was given such attention that it remained an example of the new, interventionist stance of United States policy, to be cited in much the same breath as the Soviet invasion of Afghanistan. The lack of a sense of proportion and of the political realities which brought so much Caribbean support for the operation, was cast aside. The Reagan administration was widely seen as 'adventurist'.

Other governments in Western Europe experienced a degree of 'rough handling' on the part of the USA during the 1980s. These experiences were to lead to the less certain vision of American priorities, at least from the standpoint of Western Europe. It was the Italian government's turn to feel the impact of an apparently brusque and forceful United States action in 1985. The saga of the Italian cruise liner, *Achille Lauro*—another minor affair in the relations of great states—brought mistrust and anger to the relations between the Italian and United States governments. The ship had been freed from the grip of Palestinian hijackers after negotiations and concerted action by the Italian and Egyptian governments, the latter being involved since the last port of call had been Port Said. An aircraft carrying the Palestinians, flying from Egypt, was diverted, after interception by American planes, to an Italian airbase. United States troops also landed and a tense and difficult negotiation began between the Italian and American authorities. The episode was not handled with the high level of cooperation and management of an earlier incident in 1980, when Italian specialists secured the release of the kidnapped American, General Dozier.[7]

The Italian government had again been exposed to a difference of view with the Americans on the matter of Libyan involvement in terrorism. Bombs at Rome and Vienna airports in January 1986 brought denunciations of Libyan complicity by the government of the United States. The Italian government took a different view and regarded the matter as not proven. Moreover Italian interests in Libya were considerably more significant than those of the USA. Although these events had a minor significance among the allies, they did not involve shifts in foreign policy or alignment.[8] However such incidents could not disguise concern about the foreign policy of the USA.

The luxury of public criticism of defence policy and of the major European ally was freely enjoyed. In many states governments were more cautious, but political parties, pressure groups and thousands of citizens discussed and challenged the assumptions on which policy had been based. A sharper division than at any time since 1945 occurred between governments and a significant section of public opinion. The issue was Europe and the subordination of West European interests to United States policies. The USSR escaped the public attacks because its menacing aspect was hidden. Nothing had developed in Poland to direct outcry against the Soviet Union. In Afghanistan, Soviet military embarrassment and the failure to crush the Pathan opposition, suggested weakness not strength, difficulties as much as cunning political advantage. Moreover the USSR had acquired a more human face. Eventually this was literally the case with the leadership of Mr Gorbachev, born in 1931. Even the enthusiasm of one of his predecessors, Mr Andropov, earned western praise; he enjoyed Glen Miller records—he even looked like Glen Miller, the band leader who vanished on a flight in 1944. The West discovered that Mr Brezhnev, whose regime had agreed the

Helsinki Final Document, loved the finest motor cars of West Europe, classic Rolls Royce and Mercedes Benz models. In contrast the 1980s brought to the USA a tougher, more anti-communist image. The extent to which West European and European interests in general were subordinated to those of the United States was not so clear. Minor incidents worried the public. President Reagan hinted at the possibility of fighting a limited nuclear war in Europe. It was also easily forgotten that the cruise and Pershing 2 missiles came to Europe at the request of European governments through NATO, and not only on the authority of an American President.

This public concern and political critique was focused on defence. In the Federal Republic of West Germany, there was a special political significance in the popular disquiet and protests,[9] but elsewhere the implied criticism of American policy towards Europe was the crucial element. Vigorous protest even in France was relevant because the USA was thought to threaten a nuclear catastrophe in Europe. The French protesters at Millau in 1983 were more concerned with the new American missiles than with the French independent deterrent.[10] In the United Kingdom, the political questions—Whose authority was required for the release of the missiles? What say had a British government?—became critical during the public debate over the installation, planned for December 1983. The strong element of anti-Americanism lay behind the concentration of protest on the three United States bases—Greenham Common in Berkshire, Mutlagen in West Germany and Comiso in Sicily. Further demonstrations in 1984 and 1985 included the American bases at Molesworth and Alconbury. Much more radical expression of hostility towards the USA included violence. Bombs were planted at NATO quarters in Belgium, and in West Germany where American service personnel were attacked, sustaining casualties. Although there were many other arguments tied in to the mood of concern throughout Europe, the United States and its policies were at the heart of it. In Germany there were serious political and social factors involved in the exceptionally powerful movement. In other respects the strategy of the alliance was questioned; could greater expenditure and effort on conventional arms change an excessive dependence on

American nuclear weapons? By no means all those who protested against the deployment of new missiles in 1982–85 were demanding unilateral disarmament. Many were very troubled by the Soviet arms and their nuclear weapons. But this served to underline the general and principal aim—the questioning of the role and policy of the USA.

The European anti-nuclear movements and the quite remarkable range of lobbies and pressure groups that supported them, from trade unions and churches to the association of prostitutes in Rome and students' groups, as well as political parties and factions, made a single common point. There was an equivalence of the nuclear power that held the future peace of Europe (and perhaps the rest of the world) in their control. Nuclear arms were a great leveller and, once acquired, they obliterated all other political or ideological distinctions between the USA and the USSR. The appeal of the argument was great, and millions marched, signed petitions and agitated in the years 1982–85 in most of the states of Western Europe. However, the principles of West European defence remained secure. Protest lost considerable impetus once the first missiles were deployed in December 1983, also when the Belgian and Dutch governments managed to obtain sufficient political support for a vote, legitimising the installation of cruise missiles on their soil in 1986. Governments in the Federal Republic and the United Kingdom could argue that they had been securely re-elected on programmes which had included the 'twin-track' decision and were endorsements of existing NATO strategy. In Italy only the handling of the *Achille Lauro* affair and the release of a Palestinian suspect visibly shook domestic politics and brought down the government of Signor Craxi, the coalition leader. A similar Cabinet was in office shortly afterwards and the government in Washington could see, with satisfaction, that no major shift of power or policy had actually taken place within the alliance.

There were other reasons for satisfaction with the alliance in the 1980s. Not only was the alliance secure, but an important encouragement for NATO came with the inclusion of Spain in 1982, the first new member since 1955. Enthusiastic support for Spanish membership came from the socialist leader and

Prime Minister, Felipe Gonzalez. His energetic speeches, thumping the table and sleeves rolled up at his party's congress in 1985, helped to bring a clear affirmative in 1986, when Spanish membership was the subject of a referendum. The military significance of Spanish participation was less than the political; Spain had existing agreements with the USA in particular, although a large army and important naval force added to alliance capacity on the southern flank. However, Spanish entry into the European Community and the supportive referendum strengthened the symbolic association of defence, economics and politics in Western Europe. A greater visual unity existed, closely linking these states with each other, and enhancing the role of NATO.

Whatever the more detailed weaknesses of the alliance, the questioning of strategy, the need to improve inter-operability and the size of conventional forces, a powerful argument for the future, was stability. Change threatened to be destabilising. Arguments for neutrality or non-alignment meant instability and uncertainty while other governments, not least that of the Soviet Union, assessed potential and latent political changes. The implications of future changes of government in newly non-aligned states were never clear. The alliance offered continuity and stability for its members and for other European governments, including that of the USSR. In the circumstances of safe and settled defence arrangements, built up and agreed by the NATO states, a growing number of cooperative projects had been started. These were politically significant because they encouraged defence integration. Many were successful, if expensive, and by no means all were weapons projects. A complete organisation of inter-state collaboration was in existence within NATO. The schemes in question were to do with infrastructure and supply as much as fighting systems. The entire mobilisation programmes had to be multinational, and planning and costs were shared. A conference of the National Armament Directors existed, but other groups coordinated separate cooperative projects. Into this category of collaboration came the special funding of defence programmes between member states. For example since 1964, the Federal Republic of Germany had provided defence aid to Greece, Turkey and Portugal.[11] In the 1980s many schemes already included cooperation with the newest member state, Spain. The provision of inter-allied training facilities was another successful area of alliance operation. The fundamental stability of the alliance was the context in which these many agreements were made.

In addition, the role of France within the alliance posed more problems for political scientists than for NATO planners. The French government participated in exercises, planning, and in many of the collaborative projects for weapons and other logistic systems. Although the French government under President Charles de Gaulle had withdrawn from the military command in 1966, this had left France active in all other respects. Some special independence in the development of their nuclear arms, and clear and total control over all foreign troops likely to be on their territory, had been the benefits. But cooperation had continued, especially with the British and the West Germans. Suggestions that the socialist government, elected in France in 1981, might move closer to a full military role within NATO were disappointed. No such developments occurred and the Mitterrand presidency took on the look and style of the Gaullist years, just as Mitterrand himself acquired an increasingly Gaullist appearance, if not quite the same *grandeur*. However the continuing French importance in West European defence raised hopes of a stronger European dimension to the alliance. This had been a long-standing wish of the Americans.

Institutions existed for European cooperation. In 1976, the Independent European Programme Group was formed for this purpose. The competitiveness of the European arms industry was a major concern, as was the cost of independent research, development and production. In 1984 the Ministers of the member states of the West European Union, Britain, France, the Benelux states, West Germany and Italy, decided to promote the further development of armament cooperation.[12] The aim was to enhance European unity and will in defence matters, and to go beyond the existing achievements in this area associated with the Eurogroup within NATO. Plans to create a truly West European army had failed in 1954, with the French rejection of the European Defence Community, and the failure in 1962 of the Fouchet Plan. These proposals had threatened sovereignty in a way that NATO had never done. No government was able to move in the direction of integrated defence and sacrifice independent authority in defence matters. Perhaps the pithy comment of M. Herriot in 1954, that a European army would be the *Wehrmacht,* was still relevant. Cooperation not integration remained the aim in the 1980s, and the discussion took place within the existing institutions. Furthermore, the lack of any substantial fears of Soviet aggression in Europe and a return to Cold War politics, deprived Western Europe of the obvious integrating force. More defence spending and a more intense enthusiasm for integrated defence had been the result of past Cold War tensions. These had not clearly returned in the 1980s. The most serious issue of these years in Europe was internal trouble in Poland. But the problem was essentially Polish. Poland had been affected by decline, an archaic heavy industry and a large peasant farming community living off smallholdings. This was exceptional, as was the presence of a strong Roman Catholic Church in East European states. The awesome prospect of Soviet troops in action in East Germany would have been much more destabilising and threatening, but this was unlikely in the 1980s, and had not been brought nearer by the events in Poland. Whatever the nature of Soviet actions in Afghanistan and in Africa, the menace of Cold War did not grow in Europe.

Even the tense diplomacy surrounding the deployment of intermediate-range nuclear weapons between 1982 and 1985 was defused by the Soviet return to Geneva negotiations within a year of the first cruise and Pershing 2 missiles arriving at their bases. Some relaxation of tension followed the meeting between Mr Gorbachev and President Reagan. What this meant for European integration was not clear.

There had been a new impetus in the institutions concerned with economic and political integration in West Europe in the 1970s. This did not include defence and barely covered foreign policy. There was little reason to expect that economic and political cooperation, even in the enlarged European Community, might bring integrated defence and foreign policy. Just as the advantage of the status quo for members of NATO was stability and no rocking of the boat, any major political change in European Community institutions threatened to bring instability. An extensive and coherent agreement on foreign and defence policy would constitute such a change. Therefore the limited moves in the direction of greater European integration contributed to stable international politics. Stable European international relations in the 1980s was an important result of the slow and limited integration. Détente removed the most powerful stimulus to integrated policies. The steps in the 1980s were stumbling, despite the inclusion of Spain and Portugal into an economic and political community of twelve states (from January 1986).

The period after about the year 1980 was more stable. Détente was assured by the level of East–West cooperation. The slight threat that West Europe might 'move to the left' had almost disappeared. By 1980 no Communist Party was facing an encouraging future. The socialist/communist coalition government in France, elected in 1981, had divided in August 1984. By 1986 the decline in the electoral support for the French communists was confirmed, levels of 10 per cent were hard to believe after years of popularity. In Italy, the possibility of communist participation in a coalition government, strong in the mid-1970s, had gone. A solid centre government emerged. In Spain and in Portugal, as elsewhere, the radical left was in decline. The Soviet Union was hardly initiating a successful and corrosive political drive in the West. However with fewer fears of Soviet ambitions, the drive towards unity lost its most important motor. The institutions of the European Community functioned more or less in the same way in 1985 as they had in 1975, even in 1965. Direct elections to the Parliament had been agreed, but this institution had no legislative powers and its budgetary controls were only narrowly enlarged. No major step in principle had been taken towards political unity. There was to be more majority voting in the Council of Ministers. But all such important changes were subject to national sovereignty. Mrs Thatcher, on behalf of the British government, reasserted the spirit of the Luxembourg Compromise of 1966, that national interests were paramount and determined by sovereign governments and not by majority votes in the Council of Ministers or by the European Parliament.

Although some of the more important innovations in the

Community had come from meetings of heads of state and government, the stress was on national sovereignty. The idea of a monetary union and the urging of greater political unity made in 1985, gained their force from the summit meetings. The erosion of government responsibility for decisions was minimal. The European Community became efficient and strong, but directed towards the pursuit of mutual economic self-interest and not coordinated foreign policy. Defence policy was excluded by the original terms of the agreement creating a common market. The operating principles of the Community allowed the withholding of funds (as in the case of the United Kingdom budget contributions when the Conservative government took office in 1979, until renegotiation). The possibility of dispute within the institutions was all the greater because the continuation of the bases of détente, the dialogue between East and West Europe, restricted the movement towards greater political integration. The political leaders, or most of them, urged greater unity. This had not been achieved by 1985. Political cooperation was confined to shared aims, all of them dependent on national approval. Unanimity was explicitly required for changes in the European monetary system, and when the leaders met in December 1985, no new integrating principle was agreed.

The Soviet Union and the United States regarded economic cooperation in the European Community with mixed feelings. The old Moscow view that the Community was the economic arm of NATO was a distortion. Not only did the membership of the two organisations not overlap, but much of the common Community tariff policy worked to the disadvantage of the USA. Excluded from the European food market, thwarted in attempts to coordinate trade policy, the USA found its home markets penetrated by exports from the Community. The encouragement which US governments had given to European institutions was qualified by the knowledge that the world's largest trading block had been formed. By the 1980s, the USSR had modified earlier criticism and negotiated agreements with the Community, for example over fishing rights and quotas. The government of the Soviet Union was near to according formal recognition in 1986.

One important reason for the continued existence of this

economic colossus without political clout, was the failure to develop a role in international relations beyond the economic. The member states could pursue distinct policies with no fear of intervention on matters other than economic, and the organisation posed no military threat to the Soviet Union. The potential influence of twelve European states in international politics, as opposed to international economic and trading relations, was considerable. The recommendations for a common foreign policy, originally put together by the Davignon committee, had fallen short in implementation. Only a few *ad hoc* agreements were shared by the member governments; they held a common position on the Palestinian issue and on the political future for Namibia. They were supportive of United Nations resolutions and principles in these cases. The United Kingdom obtained Community support in 1982 when at war over the Falkland Islands. Two features stood out in these agreements. They embodied no principle of foreign policy. They were simply responses to separate circumstances with no guiding concept for future action. The common agreements were solely reactive, and held no prescription for the formulation of a European foreign policy. The accumulated statements on foreign policy had no continuity and offered no understanding of how the governments should conduct themselves in international political disputes. Moreover they were confined almost totally to remote affairs, i.e. issues arising outside Europe. Even declarations of common policies on terrorism were limited, often stimulated by politics in the Middle East, and unable to clarify the fog of extradition treaties and the many bilateral agreements that existed between individual governments. No common policy was produced for many of the European issues other than broad questions that had been raised at the European conferences on security and human rights. There was, for example, no common policy towards Poland and its difficulties. It was easier to avoid so delicate a matter, and turn to international economic agreements like the development of the Lomé conventions.[13] The inertia on foreign and defence policy was deep and reassuring. There was no immediate threat in the 1980s that the European Community might produce a coherent foreign policy, a defence argument which pulled together the industrial and technical abilities of France, Britain, West Germany and the other highly developed economies of the Community. Such an achievement might well concern both the USA and the USSR, for it would be the most powerful state in the world. The 1985 European agreement on foreign policy was mild in tone. The statement concluded that the governments 'believe that a closer cooperation on questions of European security is of a nature to contribute in a fundamental way to the development of a European identity in the matter of external policy'. No indication was given on how that cooperation might be achieved.

European Community stability, like that of NATO and the Warsaw Pact, were necessary conditions for the convergence of East and West in economic and in political matters. The paradox therefore developed that Cold War and détente were required for the security of both sides of the European ideological divide and in order that the divide itself might be crossed by businessmen and trade delegations among others. All the events and testing circumstances of the previous years, even the delicate issue of missiles, were needed to bring this conjuncture about in the 1980s. No easy formula, like Cold War or détente could cover the mixture of liaison and critical opposition which characterised international relations in Europe. Détente permitted a degree of convergence that was not readily to be abandoned. There were also few reasons for the Soviet Union to destroy the accommodation that had been reached. There were many signs of Soviet willingness to encourage convergence. Assurances of goodwill kept flowing from Moscow even at the most depressing moments of Soviet-–American relations. The opening to Bonn was always left unobstructed. Contact with the West had been beneficial for all East European states. A purely 'repressive' view of Soviet action in the East had little basis in the more sophisticated reality. The Soviet authorities learned that time and caution were good allies in European politics. Guns were used in Hungary in 1956. Yet the political leader, Mr Kadar, who arrived then in the 'bandwagons of the Soviets' so to speak, was still in office in 1986. His Hungary had become accepted as the freest and most innovative economy in Eastern Europe. In 1968 in Czechoslovakia, there was no military engagement. In

Poland, the Soviet forces had not intervened directly and the Brezhnev doctrine was not invoked. A revitalised Communist Party was the centrepiece of the strategy of the Polish government after 1980. The regimes have therefore been able to make compromises on material possessions and even on consumer demand. But concessions on the immaterial possessions, like freedom, have been a different matter, especially when these included demands for plural democratic party voting and new institutions.

Neither in the East nor in the West did détente include defence. The moral was that economic and social evolution took place without change in the principles of defence policy. Territorial integrity and non-interference have been requirements, and have allowed greater East–West cooperation in other respects. The unusually stable alliance system in Europe confirmed what had been evolving for some years. Europe was no longer the dynamic centre of Cold War and détente, but had developed a special mode of international politics. The events of the 1980s established this more securely.

However, the USA are not European and their foreign and defence policies have been rapidly changed. New weapons and more flexible policies were applied in the 1980s. President Reagan spoke frequently and firmly of his impatience at seeing his state the target in all manner of attacks. The soldiers and diplomats and private citizens of the United States were kidnapped and assassinated the world over. Military installations were attacked in West Germany and off the Libyan coast. United States marines on a peace-keeping mission in Beirut were hit by an appalling explosive onslaught in 1983 (as also were French forces on the same international mission), killing over 200. Such a global victimisation required a global defence and foreign policy in the view of the Republican administration, and this need distinguished the USA from the European allies in the 1980s. The military programme, initiated by President Carter, aimed at an all-round improvement. From 1981, record defence spending included new nuclear missiles, the M-X intercontinental system, the B-1 bomber (known as the 'flying Edsel', a reference only comprehensible to advertising executives and car enthusiasts), an expanded navy and the Rapid Deployment Force. President

Reagan modified items of the programme, Congress modified others. In March 1983 the President introduced and made a solid commitment to a special programme, the Strategic Defence Initiative. This complicated idea, to make nuclear war obsolete, exposed the gulf between the United States and the European allies in NATO.

The government of the United States invited a European participation, either directly by governments or by individual companies. The British government gave a warmer welcome to the idea than any other. The French government and President Mitterrand led the rejection and the proposal to investigate some similar purely European scheme, the Eureka project. A rather mixed support was given to this idea also, although key meetings were held in London and Hanover in 1985 to discuss the future research and financing.[14] Behind the rather cautious reception of the Strategic Defence Initiative lay several European anxieties. In general these anxieties encouraged the existing questioning of defence policy and the political purpose of the alliance. There were fears that the new anti-ballistic missile system would benefit only the USA, and not afford equivalent protection to the European states. The control of the system and the research and development certainly appeared to be confined to the United States. The second fear was that the Soviet Union might be obliged to threaten the European theatre if the new system were effective, or worse, the USSR might be goaded into some pre-emptive action however risky and unlikely this might seem. If totally successful—in itself a doubtful contingency according to many commentators—SDI would render much of the Soviet arsenal ineffective. Moreover, the French and British nuclear systems would be made completely irrelevant once the defensive shield had been installed, all the more so if the Soviet Union developed its own similar system or accepted the offer of President Reagan, and shared the American research.

Finally, the possibility of the successful deployment of such an anti-ballistic missile defence intensified West German anxieties that their territory might become the European nuclear battlefield. Even the prospect of West European collaboration in the French project, the Eureka system, held some menace for Germany. The cooperation that was offered, largely from France, was essentially nuclear, and therefore meant more nuclear weapons and nuclear systems in Europe. What the Germans might prefer was never offered, that is a more comprehensive conventional defence, as far forward as possible on the East–West frontier.

Therefore the Reagan initiative encouraged the broad discussion of European and North Atlantic defence, and in many ways increased worries about war. Some Europeans indeed believed that the Strategic Defence programme made war more likely, and not less feasible as suggested by President Reagan. However, there was a stability about the relations between European states and their allies in the East and in West. In the 1980s, this was the more striking aspect, not the latent disagreements and potential fears. The Soviet Union and the United States shared their foreign and defensive policies with allies whose governments were secure and sympathetic. By the mid-1980s, there was no immediate risk of political collapse in the Warsaw Pact. Critical comments from governments like that of President Ceaucescu in Romania who had not supported the Soviet policy in Afghanistan, did not threaten Pact solidarity nor communism. His government was firmly Marxist. The discussion of a Balkan nuclear free zone, a suggestion favoured in Romania, Bulgaria and Greece, did not seriously disrupt the Pact and threaten European stability. Similarly in the West, by 1986, the USA found largely 'friendly' governments in office among the European allies. Spain voted for continued membership of NATO, the Dutch gave the government of Mr Lubbers a 10 per cent majority, and the French had voted for a centre-right coalition in March 1986.

But this stability in Europe had two major results. Stability and broad compatibility of interests both within and between alliances, removed Europe yet further from the centre of international politics. This declining importance of Europe had begun long before, but developments after 1980 emphasised the trend. The second result was the very stability allowed more freedom to question policies and the future of international relations in Europe. There was a discussion of priorities and defence policies on a totally unprecedented scale during these years. Journalists and broadcasters in all states asked fresh questions about the role and nature of the NATO alliance, and the implications of dependence on the nuclear policy of the United States. At the heart of this lively process of reappraisal was the future of Germany. In times of European stability, more questions could be asked about the future of the Federal Republic and its place in international relations.

NOTES

1. See the discussion in M. Forsyth, *Unions of States*, (Leicester U.P., 1981), 181–5.
2. In 1981 only five states had more operational robots than the Poles—Japan, USA, West Germany, Switzerland and Italy (with the restructuring of the Fiat plant). Poland had more than France and Norway, and almost twice the number operating in the United Kingdom. The most illuminating revelations came in the Italian periodical *Panorama*, 'Goldrake fa il saldatore', 5 January 1981. These investments in automated equipment were an early and obvious indicator of the debt problems of the Polish government.
3. Stephen Woolcock, *Western Policies on East-West Trade* (Royal Institute of International Affairs, London, 1982), p. 13.
4. *Le Monde*, 12 December 1985.
5. Woolcock, *op.cit.*, p. 13.
6. Italy, Spain, France, Greece and West Germany imported more from Libya than they exported. The United Kingdom and the United States were principally exporters to Libya.
7. General Dozier had been kidnapped by Red Brigade activitists. He was released after an intelligence operation and raid by the Italian specialist unit, the *gruppo di intervento speciale dei Carabinieri*. The government of the United States had been content to work with the Italians and allow them to control the operation which ended with the release of the General unharmed, and subsequent arrests of many suspected terrorists.
8. The failure of West European governments to take direct action against the state of Libya in 1986, may have encouraged the government of the United States to engage Libyan forces in the Gulf of Sirte once again after the foray in 1981. Several terrorist outrages in the Autumn of 1985 and 1986 were thought to have Libyan connection.
9. See Chapter 3, p. 96f.
10. *Le Monde* 6 and 7 August 1983. The French groups were organised partly by the Communist Party and by the *Comité pour le désarmement nucléaire en Europe*, significantly directed at European disarmament.
11. Federal Ministry of Defence, *White Paper*, 1983, p. 126, 1985, p. 360 ff.
12. The Rome Declaration on cooperation in security within the WEU was made on 27 October 1984.

13. See Chapter 4, p. 122.
14. The French government included funds for the Eureka project in the defence budgets: 1000 million francs in 1986, 1 milliard in 1987, and 1250 millions in 1988. *Le Monde*, 19 March 1986.

3 Divided Germany in the 1980s

The coherence of the two major alliances was a consequence of German politics. The Cold War had begun in Germany, with the division of Germany. Détente had received its greatest and most resourceful impetus in Germany. The world was directly affected by the changes in Germany, from the inter-zone tensions of 1946 and 1947, the Berlin access route blockade in 1948, to the *Ostpolitik* which emerged in 1970 and blossomed with treaties between the Federal Republic of Germany and its Eastern neighbours. After the building of the wall through the centre of Berlin in August 1961, a revised agreement on access and transit was made for Berlin in 1971. Although these were apparently internal changes, the important military and political positions of the two Germanys remained so significant that the implications of these events has immediate effects on other states. During the 1980s, partly as a result of earlier developments, a series of political and economic changes occurred that threatened to alter the presuppositions upon which the policies of the two German states were based. Such a prospect inevitably affected other states, but especially the USA and USSR.

The presuppositions of the foreign policy of the Federal Republic were questioned more deeply during the years 1977–1985 than at any time since the foundation of the state in 1949. All the main political parties—Christian-Democratic, Christian Social, Social-Democratic and Free-Democratic—had hitherto based foreign policy firmly on West German participation in NATO and the European Community. These pillars had permitted some differences in

87

emphasis, notably in relation to political contacts with the East, with the Soviet Union and with the German Democratic Republic. But West German security had become anchored in NATO strategy. The West Germans had gained the commitment of their allies to a forward defence of Western Europe, as far forward as possible to ensure the security of West German territory. The opening to the East, the *Ostpolitik,* which came with the government of the Social-Democratic Chancellor, Willy Brandt, did not undermine these bases so firmly laid by Konrad Adenauer. After Willy Brandt came Herr Schmidt, a vehement realist with no illusions about the nature of communism and the Soviet Union. He, more than any West European political leader, initiated the policy of 'doppel-beschluss', the twin-track decision adopted by the NATO Ministers in 1979, to deploy the American intermediate-range cruise and Pershing 2 missiles in West Europe, and to seek further arms limitation and control talks with the Soviet Union. Governments in the Federal Republic had not been divided on the principles of foreign and defence policy. A remarkable consensus was therefore broken when these issues were questioned during the 1980s.

There were several reasons why such a questioning should have begun and why it had an immediate political impact. Changes in the nuclear arsenals of both the Soviet Union and the United States were part of the reason, but more profound changes had been taking place that allowed and encouraged the reappraisal that began about 1979. To many observers outside Germany, especially perhaps to politicians, the great increase in economic links between the Federal Republic and the states of the East and the Soviet Union which occurred in the 1970s, was the most striking factor.

Several western states had benefited from the growth in trade and investment between their economies and those of the closed economic systems of Eastern Europe, but the Federal Republic had benefited most. West German banks and businesses did more East trade than those of any other country, and they invested more. This had grown rapidly in the years of *Ostpolitik* and with détente between the USA and USSR. A convergence of economies had been created, a new degree of inter-dependence. For the Eastern states there was a chance to obtain, in a secure and orderly manner, the goods and materials that they desired, as well as important investment in their developing economies. For the West the benefit was the maintenance of production, particularly after 1973 with a recession provoked by the increase in the price of oil. This had helped to prevent even worse unemployment, and the significantly better performance of the Federal Republic than its European partners in employment, inflation and production in the decade 1974–84 was partly assisted by the 'Ost-handel', the trade with the East.

The argument for the development of such trade was not that there would be an erosion of the principles of the closed economies of the East and thus an erosion of communism. For the majority of West Germans the advantages were quite pragmatic. The demand existed, and was increasing with the rapid rate of technical innovation of these years. The West Germans no doubt sold the essential trivia of consumer life to the states of the East, but above all they dealt in major projects. Their banks and industries were involved in the work on the infrastructure, building airports, road and rail communications, factory installations and grid systems. West German firms had the largest foreign element in the construction of the pipelines, storage and pumping stations for the Siberian natural gas project which came to fruition in the early 1980s. Many banks from the West had a considerable investment in the East, for example the *Commerzbank* and the *Bank für Gemeinwirtschaft* had major credit arrangements in Poland in 1981 and 1982, as did the *Hessische Landesbank*. There were suggestions in the press that German companies and banks were the major creditors of the Hungarian government and had financed the programme of economic liberalisation that had taken place. By a curious irony it seemed that the economic and fiscal policies of Hitler's Third Reich had been unwittingly achieved by the Federal Republic, but without the desire to bring political influence to bear on the states of the East.

Although the Federal Republic's citizens traded with all states in the East, and very extensively with the Soviet Union, it was with the German Democratic Republic that the largest amount was done. East–West German trade was not included within the European Community external tariff arrangements. This was regarded as an inter-German matter and therefore excluded. A true figure for that trade was impossible to reach and never clearly quoted. The evidence was, however, available for all to see at the road and rail frontiers between the two Germanys. This added to the level of interdependence between West Germany and the states of the East. No West German government could lightly risk the loss of such contracts. By 1981 some estimates were suggesting as many as 1.5–2 million jobs depended on trade and investment with economies in the East. In the case of trade with the Democratic Republic, there was also an emotional factor. Many West Germans argued that their compatriots in the East were still suffering for the events of 1933–45, the agony brought upon much of the world by German politics. In the Federal Republic, the debt had been paid, but not in the East and it was incumbent on West Germans to assist those in the East. They could best do this through investment and commerce.[1]

Much of this passed either unnoticed or did not receive exceptional attention among the allies and partners of the Federal Republic. What began to concern others, particularly the government of the United States, was the political significance of this trade. There were two aspects: the continuing expansion of economic ties with the East European states might create an important level of dependence, and thus influence foreign and defence policy; in addition the leverage thus created might be put to use, trying to influence Soviet policy. This has been latent in the kind of economic embargo suggested by President Carter. It became open when President Reagan came to power. West European governments refused to follow his lead in applying economic sanctions to the Soviet Union following the invasion of Afghanistan and the threat of action and intervention in Poland in 1982 and again in 1983. The Federal Republic had followed the lead of the USA in 1980 in boycotting the Olympic Games in Moscow. Trade sanctions were not applied, then or later. The charge that there was already too great a dependence upon trade with the Eastern bloc was rebutted. American critics suggested that the participation of German and other West European firms in the building of the natural gas link from Siberia and the proposals that such gas should be supplied to West Europe, were examples of this dependence, and were rejected. The energy dependence on Soviet gas was minimal. In the last resort, the Federal Republic could find other sources.[2]

Moreover the position was more complicated. European governments had been aware of the dangers of too close and too extensive economic links with the East. Levels of trade had begun to fall long before the Soviet invasion of Afghanistan. The high points were reached in the mid-1970s and there had been a decline or at most some fluctuation around similar levels in value and volume since then. In the case of the Federal Republic the evolution of trade with the East showed no possibility of extending dependence. In 1979 the total trade value, according to OECD and UN figures, of imports and exports between the Federal Republic and the entire Soviet bloc states was *c.* 10 per cent of the total European Community trade of the Republic.[3] By 1983 the value of the trade had dropped. Despite a small increase in trade with the Soviet Union, Eastern bloc trade was only 9 per cent of the value of European Community trade, which had also declined. The trade between the Federal Republic and East European states other than the USSR had fallen by 33 per cent in the same four years. There was little risk of serious dependence growing in this commerce.

The significance of the economic relationship which had developed between the Federal Republic of Germany and all of the states of Eastern Europe was quite different. The lack of any danger of dependence and ties was precisely the significant point. Because there was no risk of bowing to Soviet political demands or rejecting NATO policies in order to keep an exceptionally profitable two-way trade, a new freedom entered West German policy. The Republic had become a bridge, safe in its position in Europe, but a bridge between West and East Europe. The political importance of trade with the East lay in the fact that West Germans could indulge in it without risk to their political system or loyalties. Where there was any danger of 'playing into Soviet hands', the government in Bonn would back down, as had been the case with trade in certain goods which might have military uses. Some new categories of such sensitive commodities, especially in the computer and electronics fields, were placed under a prohibition and could not be exported to the East. But in general the political stature of the Federal Republic grew with the knowledge that the economic relationship with the East had not fundamentally altered German policy.

While nothing irrevocable came with economic links with East, there were also important social ties between the Federal Republic and Eastern Europe. For many West Germans the link was essentially between their state and the German Democratic Republic. The depth of the contacts between the peoples of the two Germanys became the basis for a different political relationship, and this factor also encouraged a questioning of the assumptions behind West German policies.

No West German politician could afford to ignore the reality of inter-German relations. Although there had been emigration from the East since 1945, and that flow had declined, especially since the later 1950s and the building of the Berlin wall in 1961, the social fact was ever-present and ever-pressing. By the 1980s there was an accumulation of contact and inter-German experience that had special significance for foreign and defence policy. Although the movement of thousands across the East–West German border had stopped, a few people still managed to flee across the armed and guarded frontiers between the two Germanys. Within Berlin there were still a number of methods of crossing. Others were released by the administration of East Germany. This number was larger in 1984 and 1985 than in the years immediately before, some of whom were 'bought' by the West German government. Funds were available for such transactions. A welcome and financial help existed in the Federal Republic for those who emigrated from the East; older people were able to claim pension rights in the West and were thus encouraged to cross. There was no possibility that contact between the two Germanys would be less, despite the different social systems. The links were forged again and again by the movement of peoples, and by the fact that others remained behind. Therefore relations between governments responded to the social realities, and formal diplomatic exchanges allowed further agreements during the 1970s. The four-power agreement over access in Berlin, between the British, French and American sectors on the one hand, and the Soviet–East German part of the city on the other, was signed in 1971 and extended in 1972. This permitted recognition of the German Democratic Republic without compromising the military commissariat which had administered Berlin since 1945, and was endorsed by both German states. Such measures brought tangible results for ordinary Germans. It became easier to travel to the East, and also relatively easier to travel to the West. Trade and other delegations moved more freely. Families found that some of the obstacles to their meetings were removed. By the mid-1980s, it was possible for many more visits to be made by West Germans to relatives in the East. This was especially beneficial for those living within 100 km of the inner-German frontier. Although an entry charge was raised by the Democratic Republic (25 DM had to be exchanged at the crossing-point) this did not deter the flow of people. In 1982, 13 million cars crossed from West to East, and 525 million DM were exchanged in this 'transit' traffic. For many people in both East and West Germany, the achievement of détente and of *Ostpolitik* was the making easier of communications with their own families—in some cases, with the land of their birth.

The development of links between the two Germanys bore the appearance of a narrowing of the differences. This was misleading. The process was not irreversible and should not be exaggerated. The flow of visitors across the inner German frontier began to decline slightly in 1984 and 1985. The principal reason was financial. The cost of visits did not end with the 25 DM levy at the crossing-point. The realities of such visits imposed major financial burdens on Germans from the Federal Republic. The high standard of living which they enjoyed placed a moral obligation upon many of them to bring presents and to leave often large amounts of their valuable currency behind with their friends and relations. The access which foreign currency provided to consumer goods was increasingly marked. Electrical goods or even a motor car became available within days with the supply of western currency. Without such funds, these items would take years to acquire in some cases. The hidden costs of easier communications between the two Germanys inhibited the traffic that it was intended to encourage. It was cheaper to enjoy a fortnight on the Mediterranean than a week in the Democratic Republic for many citizens of the Federal Republic. But many still made the journey, especially those living within 100 km of the border for whom special and easier travel conditions were negotiated. The sense of moral obligation owed to the less fortunate Germans living in the East gave this communication its political significance.

There was nothing here of reunification. Although the issue was presented as an aim in the constitution of the Federal Republic and was a NATO commitment, the social contacts had not led to a demand for reunification. In many respects the aim was more of an embarrassment than a real policy. Other aspects of communication between the two Germanys were also awkward. A strange twilight world of influence and spying existed. The motive might be money, but the possibility of interpenetration on either side of the inner German border conveyed some sense of common identity and shared experience. The very uniqueness of the German condition was a cause for remark and questioning of policies. All manner of Germans had been approached and in some cases lured across the frontier in both directions. While the Soviet Union and the United States exchanged spies, and occasionally 'dissidents', the two Germanys exchanged only Germans.

The close relationship between the two Germanys, and the growing trade with the East European states in general, provided the background and the special circumstances in which a revision of foreign and defence policies might occur. The change in government in the Federal Republic, from a Social-Democratic and Free Democratic coalition to a Christian-Democratic and Free Democratic coalition, and the success of the new grouping in the 1983 elections, encouraged the discussion of German security and was indeed partly caused by that discussion. A debate had begun in the political parties and in the country over the security of the Republic. The Social-Democrats were to move away from the NATO policy supported by Helmut Schmidt in 1979, the twin-track decision. Although the party never went so far as to recommend the withdrawal from NATO, the possibility was on the agenda for debate. In 1985 this became less likely with the support given to Johannes Rau, party leader for the period up to the next legislative elections in 1987. Nevertheless, the opposition party was able to enjoy the luxury of such an open debate, and this was reflected in the passionate consideration of foreign and defence policy. The Green Party, which obtained 27 seats in the 1983 elections, had an anti-nuclear and anti-NATO platform. The fact of elections in 1983 therefore encouraged the intense preoccupation with foreign and defence matters which characterised West Germany in the 1980s. No actual change of policy occurred since the governing majority was secure; Helmut Kohl and the Christian-Democratic Union, with the Christian Social Party and the Free Democrats, had a large share of the vote and the seats.[4] Herr Genscher, the Free Democrat, was a firm supporter of the existing policies and of the decision to accept American cruise and Pershing 2 missiles in West Germany. Thus while the governing coalition held to one policy, a radical debate which had begun earlier, continued in West Germany.

The core of the matter was the security of the state. The questioning of policy was stimulated by the fear of war and the renewed fear of a nuclear war in Europe. The German experience had been exceptional. Many European states had suffered physical destruction on a similar scale, though few were blistered so completely. Only the Soviet Union suffered comparable casualties. Political destruction followed. No other state was so mauled by division and the necessary humiliation of military government. A break with tradition and with German history was sought by the victors when new political institutions were created to take over from the military administrations. The political and administrative units of the new Germany, the *Länder*, for the most part bore little connection with older components. Hamburg and Bremen were totally rebuilt; only Bavaria and the Saarland had historical roots which ran directly to the new *Länder*. In the East, the Soviet zone which became East Germany had few links with the past, despite de Gaulle's gibe that the Democratic Republic was merely Prussia and Saxony. The redirection of economic energies also helped to transform the previously rural area into a major industrial state.

In this restructured Germany, with its frontiers hacked about and its great industry smashed or removed to the East in the years 1945–47, its former capital city divided and isolated geographically and politically, fear of another war cut deeply into the minds of all German generations. A war from the West seemed unlikely to Germans in the Federal Republic, and the achievement of Konrad Adenauer was to tie the new Republic to Western Europe. Forward defence became the only acceptable military doctrine for the NATO states once Germany had become a member of the alliance in 1955. Any revision of the strategy which contemplated fighting a war further west would render the participation of the Federal Republic a nonsense. By 1980 two developments had affected the assessment of the likelihood of war in Germany. The first was the declining fear of a Soviet attack, despite the vast forces gathered to the east of the inner-German border. NATO strength had not deteriorated and the creation of a respected West German army and a revived and efficient defence industry, helped to place the fear of a Soviet invasion in a calmer context. The second factor was the proliferation of nuclear weapons in Europe.

Fears of a war unleashed by the USSR gave way to fears of war caused by accidental release of weapons or the pressure of events leading to the release of such nuclear weapons. The moment came for the flowering of these fears in 1979 and 1980, with the NATO decision to instal cruise and Pershing 2 missiles in Western Europe, with both types of missiles in the Federal Republic. The Soviet deployment of their SS missiles had not attracted such attention because there was little prospect that Moscow would pay any attention. Also a furore was created by the revelation that the United States were investing in a 'neutron' bomb, an enhanced radiation weapon which would destroy people but not buildings. Germany seemed to be the focus of such weapons. On these fears an important groundswell of opinion was created which gained extra impetus in 1979 and into the 1980s because the new American weapons were not to be deployed until December 1983. However by 1983, the movement had involved some 3–4 million West Germans. All manner of occupational and professional groups made a commitment to seek the removal of the weapons and a change of policy. They demonstrated at the American base at Mutlagen. On 5 October, 1983 West

German workers attempted a national protest, a five-minute interruption of work. Although the protest was unevenly followed, the trade union organisation was in support of the protest. 560,000 Federal government employees signed a petition against the NATO policy, and on the back of this public feeling the Green Party gained its electoral successes at *Land* and at national levels.

The intensity of the West German peace movement was not equalled in other states. However a considerable wave of public opinion was mobilised, yet no government changed its policy, although in the Netherlands and in Belgium, wavering changes of coalition government and delays affected the timing of the deploying of the missiles. The protests in all other NATO states took a lead from West Germany. Only there were both types of missile in Germany, and protests there were generally larger than those elsewhere. But the cumulative effect of thousands of West Europeans demonstrating against the installation of new nuclear weapons at Greenham Common airbase in Berkshire, Comiso in Sicily, as well as in Germany, created a formidable sense of direction and purpose. Political parties were not untouched in 1983, and in many states several parties began to reinforce the criticism of NATO policy. In the Federal Republic, the former Chancellor Herr Schmidt was all but isolated in 1984 among the Social-Democrats. However there were important differences in the nature and significance of the protest movement in West Germany. The implications of the movement held a deeper meaning than protests in the United Kingdom, Italy or in Belgium and the Netherlands. Demands for a revision of the defence policy of the Federal Republic automatically suggested a complete revision of the security of the Republic and indeed of the West. Where policies of convergence and détente had meant economic relations and discussion of arms controls for other states in Western Europe, these policies implied the reorientation of foreign and defence policy for the Federal Republic.

By the 1980s, and perhaps much earlier, many Germans were less convinced of the real threat of Soviet invasion. Too many obstacles obviously stood in the way of such a menace. The certainty of military retaliation was only one of these, although possibly the most serious obstacle. Not only the weapons of the

United States and the United Kingdom threatened the USSR, but also those of France as well as the total strength of the NATO divisions. Political uncertainties in Eastern Europe and social confusion in West Germany in the eventuality of a European war, both served as deterrents to aggression. But all such arguments depended on evaluations that might change. What had definitely changed was the atmosphere of fear and suspicion that once existed between the Soviet Union and the West Germans. This had not totally vanished, but a *modus vivendi* had appeared, based on the daily communication on economic and social issues. Therefore the advantages of détente for the Federal Republic were great. They were not to be abandoned lightly. The fear of nuclear war and the need to protect the benefits which had come from détente and *Ostpolitik* were the predominant German emotions. Thus there were real arguments for considering a reorientation of policies. Security to the West was assured by Federal German participation in NATO and in the European Community. There might be an argument for seeking a secure future by an accommodation with the East.

However no West German government had contemplated the step. As the prospect of elections drew nearer, the policy statements and speeches from the Social-Democrats became less radical in 1985. Their designated leader, Johannes Rau, was no radical firebrand, demanding withdrawal from the alliance. But changes of opinion had occurred which no government could ignore. The old policies on which there had been such consensus now required ever clearer explanations and justifications. In 1986 any accommodation with the USSR seemed fanciful, yet such a policy had attractions. In its extreme form, such a policy might mean a demilitarised and/or neutral Germany, both sides of the inner German frontier. This might be a step-by-step process removing some of the nuclear weapons at the outset. The prize, long desired by the Soviet Union, would be the end to their fears of the re-emergence of a strong, armed Germany. Such a policy would also remove the Soviet fear that a loss of West German confidence in the United States, would lead to the development of an independent German nuclear arsenal. Any undermining of NATO strategy, including the nuclear policy, invited the consideration of some such security arrangement with the USSR. After all, there were several precedents. These had also seemed unlikely months and even days before some of the diplomatic agreements were announced. This certainly applied to the most notorious treaty, the Ribbentrop—Molotov Pact of 23 August 1939. There had been others, dating from Bismarck's Reinsurance Treaties between the German and Russian Empires of the 1880s, to the Treaty of Rapallo in 1922, and the Treaty of Berlin, in 1926, the so-called 'Eastern Locarno'. All achieved the same apparent benefit for Russia and Germany—a defined relationship and greater security. In many respects these hopes were illusory, but they were not necessarily so. Indeed some have argued that the very failure of the Kaiser to reaffirm the earlier treaties with Russia after 1890, led indirectly to the sense of insecurity and the war of 1914.

Pressures for such a major reorientation were not great in the 1980s. However there had been enough change and concern in German public opinion for any hint of a review of NATO commitments by other member states to have reverberations in the Federal Republic. The British government, for example, had been known to have considered troop reductions from the British Army of the Rhine. Such a policy might have encouraged uncertainties among West Germans, and turned more eyes towards a revised security policy, guaranteed by the Soviet Union. On the other hand, the USSR had every reason to encourage the Federal Republic to move in the direction of a revised treaty relationship. Anything was preferable to a nuclear weapon, controlled independently by a German government.[5] But this was speculation in the mid-1980s. Only the basic ingredients were present for the Soviet Union to consider what one German commentator has called 'playing the German card'.[6] The most important ingredient was the way in which the West Germans looked at their own security from another European war, a war likely to be fought with nuclear weapons.

The strategic position of Germany and the unusual political pressures which developed especially in the years after 1979 and the NATO decision to deploy new missiles, amounted to a questioning of German identity. The place of Germany, West Germany above all, as the battlefield for any future European war concentrated attention on this question. There was a sense in which the penalty for Nazism and the Second World War was still exacted through the threat of war, fought on the central front according to a doctrine of forward defence, that is fought in West Germany. This threat, and the hope that Germans might clutch at that other strand in their history and appeal to European pacificism and internationalism, brought different German generations together in the search for a new German identity. Contemporary Germans were certainly good Europeans and were accepted as such by other West European peoples. But in this as in defence, West Germans followed and participated, they did not initiate and lead. There was therefore no place for the state of West Germany, one of the most stable and prosperous democracies of the world. No sovereign political role stood out, commensurate with the economic strength of the Federal Republic. Under the particular impact of the placing of both Soviet and American intermediate range nuclear weapons in Europe and in both Germanys, the demand for their removal and the questioning of foreign policy suggested just such a role. Germany might stand as a political bridge between East and West as it stood already as the geographical bridge. In this respect an element of European impartiality was appropriate, committed to European unit first, rather than to one side or the other. French observers of Germany were among the first to point out this thirst for a political identity, but it was firmly expressed also in Germany.[7] The idea that conveyed the sense of a new political responsibility was the common fate of the Federal Republic and that of the German Democratic Republic.

In 1984 the cruise and Pershing 2 missiles had arrived in the Federal Republic. Part of the Soviet response was the deployment of SS 20 missiles in the German Democratic Republic later the same year. They were also to be stationed in Czechoslovakia. This development fuelled the belief that the two Germanys were victims of superpower policies and the strategies of their respective alliances. They shared the role of victim and probable battleground. The missiles not only bore a physical resemblance, they sharpened the sense of German identity. Certainly political satire was quick to make the point that there was an equivalence of policy on the part of both alliances. In Berlin, home of German wit and satire and the junction of East and West, the two Germanys shared the description of 'Kein schönes Land' ('no attractive country') in the title of a current political review.[8] Links between the protest movement against the stationing of new missiles from West Germany and those from the East were at least attempted in 1984 and 1985. But the question of intermediate range missiles was only a kind of catalyst. The deeper trend was the sense and awareness of a common fate. Even the hedonistic weekly picture magazines of the West showed a concern that the real benefits of détente and *Ostpolitik*, the easier communication between Germans on both sides of the inner German border, might be threatened by new policies.[9] The presence of many Germans who had come over from the East enhanced this shared awareness. Such contact was symbolised by the efforts of Wolf Biermann, a popular singer and guitarist, Dr Havemann and Rudolph Bahro, and was encouraged by the appeals of Bishop Hempel of the Evangelical Church. The argument was not about reunification but about a common sympathy and fate.

The extensive contacts between the two Germanys was the essential factor in the 1980s. These had long existed, but never so intensely felt nor pursued.

The basis of the common identity was the emphasis on a common history. There were important opportunities for this during the 1980s. In 1983 the 500th anniversary of the birth of Martin Luther was celebrated in both Germanys. The acceptance of German tradition by the Marxist regime in the East came with a celebration of Prussian history, a kind of East German voyage of discovery. All of these roots were common to both East and West, and they were essentially German. But there was no neglect of the fact of the different social systems, and the possibility of reunification was not associated with this historical appreciation. Indeed there remained a demand by West Germans that the part of Berlin in the control of the three western allied states since 1945 should be more fully integrated into the Federal Republic. This demand became more firmly voiced in the 1980s. The focus was not the removal of the allied military presence but the application of Federal law and greater freedom of communication between the Federal Republic and

West Berlin. In 1985 and 1986 Lufthansa, the West German airline, requested that it might be allowed to fly direct to Berlin. This had not been accepted before, and only Air France, British Airways and PanAm flew between airports in the Federal Republic and West Berlin. Berlin, the largest industrial city of Germany, was in effect legally and politically excluded from either Germany.[10] In the Western part of the city, allied military law remained in force as it had done since 1945. The significance was all the greater because Berlin had been the capital city in the period of union and Empire. Berlin was part of the German identity. All these issues were in the forefront of German politics in the 1980s.

The political implications of reappraisal of policies was not confined to the Federal Republic and to a certain historical nostalgia on the part of the German Democratic Republic. There was a great stress placed upon the continuity of inner German affairs by the government and the Socialist Unity Party leadership in the East. Although the much anticipated visit by Herr Honecker to the Federal Republic was postponed in 1984, apparently on the authority of the Soviet Union, this was merely a minor hiccup in relations. The visit was still expected in 1986 and, were it to occur, formed one of a series of important political exchanges between senior men on both sides. These had become well established and included politicians other than those in government. The Social-Democratic leader, Herr Rau had paid such a visit in 1985, as had Franz Joseph Strauss, the Bavarian Christian Social Party leader and Minister-President, in 1984. Herr Strauss had been a vehement critic of the communist regime and an opponent of many of the details of *Ostpolitik* for many years. Yet, by the 1980s, even he recognised the necessity of making such a visit. Moreover he was also a supporter of economic exchange between the two Germanys and his visit brought further negotiations on the matter of West German credits for major projects in the East. The nature of political contacts between Germans had a strange dualism. On the one hand, were the hard economic realities of the developing commerce between the two states. On the other, was a delicate expression of German identity. It had been rumoured that the climax of the proposed visit by Herr Honecker was to be a trip to the Saarland from which his family originated.

The foreign and defence policies of the Federal Republic reached a special point in the 1980s, clearly sensed by the political leaders of both Germanys. There was no intention by either government of abandoning their alliance obligations. Both states remained firmly rooted in quite alien social systems. As long as their allies showed no wavering in their commitments to the defence and security of both Germanys, no change seemed likely, despite the unprecedented levels of public criticism and debate, particularly in the Federal Republic. But there was also a new emphasis. In the West this took the form of growing confidence in the capacity and need for the Federal Republic and its inhabitants to be able to look both westwards, as they had done since the foundation of the state, and eastwards, as the history of Germany dictated. Nowhere was this more clearly stated than in the Federal Republic's own Defence White Paper, in 1985. The defence policy, and the total commitment to NATO and the cause of free political institutions, was fully set out in that document. However, there was also a new dimension, not included in the Defence White Paper of 1983, for example. This envisaged a special task for the Federal Republic, giving expression to many of the trends and suggestions that had been made during the 1980s. The crucial paragraph (para. 39) was quite explicit about the importance of this aspect of Federal policy:

The Federal Goverment's policy towards the German Democratic Republic is an integral part of its policy for peace rooted in the Western Alliance. Both German history and the present political and geographic constellations confer a special responsibility on the two German states for peace and stability in the heart of Europe. The policy of dialogue with the GDR is a contribution of the Federal Republic of Germany to active NATO policy for peace in Europe. But it is also an effort to ease the hardships resulting from the division of Germany and to enhance the feelings of Germans belonging together as a nation as long as reunification by self-determination continues to be denied them. Since October 1982, new impulses and initiatives had made it possible to achieve practical benefits for people in both parts of Germany.[11]

The context in which this new impetus was placed was that of the Helsinki Accord. Although the significance of the Conference on Cooperation and Security was directed towards confidence-building measures between the western allies and the member states of the Warsaw Pact, and also towards the many cases of individual suffering or hardship, for the Federal Republic there was an additional importance. The agreement brought new hopes for European cooperation and thus links between the two Germanys acquired a particular significance. For the United Kingdom, among other governments and states of Europe, the Helsinki process was hardly a step in the direction of improved inter-German relations. For the government in Bonn, however, the Helsinki Final Act, the improving relations between East and West Germany and the economic and other contacts which had followed the treaties with the governments of Eastern Europe in the early 1970s, was all part of the same process, that of freeing communication and dialogue within Europe, essential to the peace of the continent. Such policy required firm support from the allied governments.

This support was necessary not only for the political reason that the German reorientation rested on the cohesion of NATO. There were growing pressures on the German defence policy as a result of manpower shortages. Predictions for the later years of the decade and for the last decade of the century suggested that the conscripted Federal army would have to expect some 90,000 fewer recruits and conscripts. The Federal Republic had the lowest birth rate in Europe and there had been a decline in the total population since the 1960s.[12] Indeed the West Germans had the lowest 'gross reproduction rate' in Europe and there seemed little statistical reason for optimism about a different, or reversal of the trend before the end of the century.[13] Yet the Republic provided the largest land army in NATO's European front. Any alteration in the policy of the other major member states would threaten to confuse and complicate the defence options. All the political factors and pressures indicated a need to provide a stable and secure background for the evolution of the foreign policy of the Federal Republic. However the Federal Ministry of Defence was hopeful that measures taken in 1984 would prevent the threatened fall in manpower from 495,000 to 300,000.[14] Moreover the security of Western European states and the maintenance of a strategy of forward defence, as near as feasible to the inner German border, required no major change in the manpower and reinforcement plans of other NATO states.

In the last twenty years of the twentieth century there were therefore an increasing number of uncertainties surrounding those who had to formulate the foreign and defence policies of the Federal Republic. Germany remained the vital element in European politics, no longer hemmed in by other states, but increasingly ready to take initiatives. Whenever German politics was uncertain and central to European security, one state before all others was immediately concerned: the USSR.

Since 1945, the Soviet Union had seen only a relative expansion of German power. Two German states had appeared and had begun to develop an understanding and a shared experience. East Germany was an exceptionally stable socialist economy. The predominantly rural character of that part of Germany before the Second World War had been changed into a structured and successful industrial economy. In the West, the Federal Republic had become an economic giant among capitalist states, rivalled only by Japan and the USA in its productivity and innovative and marketing energies. The Republic had become the major trading partner of the Soviet Union and the entire Eastern bloc in the free-market world. In 1955 the Soviet Union had suffered the incorporation of the Federal Republic into NATO and its armies faced more Germans than any other nationality across the border in Central Europe. The West German army was once again the largest army in Europe other than that of the USSR. By the 1970s, the navy of the Federal Republic had ships to send outside the European waters of the North Sea and the Baltic, in support of British and other navies in the Red Sea and the area around the Persian Gulf as well as on goodwill missions further afield. Nuclear weapons, albeit in the control of the United States, were stationed on West German soil, and increasingly so. There had been few developments from the point of view of the USSR that could have been described as re-assuring as far as Germany was concerned since 1945. By the 1980s the West Germans had developed a flourishing and prosperous defence industry, supplying NATO forces with equipment as well as those of many other states, especially the booming Brazilian defence industry. Technology offered no obstacles for the West Germans; the question had to be increasingly asked in the Soviet Union—at what point and under what conditions would the Federal Republic secure its ultimate defence and possess nuclear capability?

From the Soviet point of view the consideration of German policy was more urgent in the 1980s. The possibility of German control of nuclear weapons did not decrease. This was a perpetual fear and the basis of latent mistrust between the East European states and Germany. Détente accentuated this mistrust because it did not change the relationship between Germany and Europe. Federal Germany had not, of course, dominated Western Europe. Even without the presence of the United States, France, the United Kingdom and Italy built powerful defences and their military production and holdings of military equipment far exceeded those of the Federal Republic. West Germany was one state among equals in NATO. France and Britain possessed nuclear arms. Although the economic strength of the Federal Republic was formidable, it could not challenge the combined economic resources of the European Community states. But the political balance never looked quite so secure from east of the Iron Curtain. The strength of Federal Germany had a different potential. Only the USSR had a more impressive economy and a greater military capacity. The rapid industrial progress of the German Democratic Republic outstripped that of other Warsaw Pact states but lagged far behind that of its German neighbour. The Federal Republic had a population of some 55 million, despite the lowest birth rate in the world. Apart from the Soviet Union, no state in the Warsaw Pact had a population of anything like that size, let alone the resources of mind and market place, and the skills. Only Poland, with almost 30 million people, possessed a substantial population. But many of these inhabitants were occupied in the declining heavy industries of steel, coalmining and shipbuilding, often run with outmoded machinery and organisation, or in fragmented, poor agricultural units. The frantic attempts to modernise the factories and introduce new industry has led to the vast foreign debts, often from West Germany, contracted during the 1970s. These indirectly contributed to the demands for a reorganisation of the administration. By 1980 the Polish government was in economic and political difficulties. None of the other states had a population of more than 20 million, and both Hungary, with about 10 million, and Bulgaria, were very small by

European standards. The armed forces of the Warsaw Pact were correspondingly small. The total armed forces of the Pact, excluding those of the Soviet Union, were scarcely larger than those of the Federal Republic. The concept of the 'citizen in uniform' was retained in West Germany, and associated with an extensive programme of political and leadership training, and the presentation of the values of society to the young recruits and conscripts, known by the untranslatable title of 'Innere Führung'. This had created an impressive force by 1980. The fear of this imposing neighbour had deep roots, and nothing that had occurred since 1945 was completely re-assuring. The need to avoid potential German domination of the living space between the Elbe and the Soviet frontier had not disappeared. The Soviet Union had always feared such German domination. Thus the necessity for a clear delineation of mutual interest had not gone with the division of Germany, and Soviet need for security became greater than before. Its interests were jealously guarded.

The USSR retained a tight grip on all aspects of military security. This was vital in so far as the strategic balance seemed to be working against their interests in the 1980s. A more forceful administration in the United States had come forward with proposals for stronger defence. Few secure allies had appeared in Africa, Latin America or in Asia. Although there were some signs of improving relations between the USSR and the People's Republic of China, as noted by Mr Gorbachev in his speech on the occasion of the Soviet Communist Party Congress in 1986, the major movement in foreign policy by the Chinese government was for more agreements with Japan and the United States. Relations between the Chinese government and that of the United Kingdom on the future of Hong Kong were settled by an agreement in 1984. It was therefore investment, trade and technical assistance from western economies that came to the People's Republic during the 1980s and not principally from the Soviet Union, While the Soviet Union expanded its fleet in the Pacific, the United States developed commercial ties and the Far East and Pacific became the fastest growing region for American commerce during the decade after withdrawal of troops from Vietnam. There were therefore growing pressures on the USSR to welcome any political agreement that might offer stability and security, and the evolution of the politics of the Federal Republic held both menace and fascination. The menace was clear; the Republic was armed and the centrepiece of the NATO strategy. The fascination came from the possibility of a reorientation of policies as the century drew to a close and the shadow of Nazism and the Second World War receded for Germans if not for Russians. For the USSR the basis of European policy was the 'principle that the danger of war must never emanate from German soil again'.[15] That basic principle could only be realised through a policy of convergence, 'establishing cooperation' and 'constructive cooperation between the former allies, among all states',[16] as Mr Gorbachev stressed in a message to the Soviet and American veterans who met on the Elbe in 1985.

The Federal Republic of Germany therefore regained a central position in international politics. However the direction of German policies depended in great measure on the nature of the alliances that had existed in Europe since the height of the cold war after 1945. These in turn depended upon the fate of the superpowers. Soviet and United States policies had to take into account a more extensive world, and one in which a new internationalism carried some impact, the internationalism of economic interdependence.

NOTES

1. Some exceptionally large credit arrangements were negotiated in the 1980s, including a 1 milliard DM credit with no formal ties— some earlier arrangements had been conditional on the purchase of West German goods. Even the strongly anti-communist leader of the Bavarian Christian Social Party, Franz Joseph Strauss, went to the Democratic Republic and discussed further credit arrangements in 1984 since the Bavarian *Landesbank* was an important participant in the deal.
2. In the years 1983–85 West European dependence on natural gas from the USSR grew from 10 per cent of total consumption to 19 per cent. Thus the Russians had become the second largest single supplier, ahead of the United Kingdom (17 per cent) and Algeria (16 per cent). In 1984 overall consumption of natural gas grew by more than 7 per cent over the 1983 level. *Times*, 10 January 1986, and *Le Monde*, 29 January 1985 provided full surveys.
3. United Nations *International Trade Statistics*, vol. 1 (New York, 1985).

4. The governing coalition had 278 of the 498 seats in the West German Parliamentary Lower House, the *Bundestag*. The percentage of the vote won by the coalition parties was 55 per cent.
5. There had been rumours of West German collaboration with Israel in nuclear testing in Zaire in the 1980s.
6. Dr Heinz Schulte of *Europaarchiv*.
7. Prof. Alfred Grosser, writing in *Le Monde*, 24 November 1983.
8. *Die Stachelschweine*.
9. *Quick*, January 1984.
10. Although West Berlin sent members to the *Bundesrat* in Bonn, they did not have the voting rights of the representatives of the other Federal *Länder*.
11. *White Paper*, p. 20-1.
12. Maurice Kirk (ed.), *Demographic and Social Change in Europe 1975–2000* (Liverpool U.P., 1981), p. 6.
13. *Ibid.*, p. 152. The West German rate was lower than those for Sweden and Denmark.
14. *White Paper* (1985), p. 237 ff.
15. *Recalling the Past for the Sake of the Future* (Moscow, 1985), p. 126.
16. Quoted in the press on the occasion, and *ibid.*, p. 130.

4 The Second New International Economic Order

The fate of the world seemed to lie as firmly as ever in the hands of the two leaders of the two most powerful states in the 1980s. Yet life itself must have seemed as securely tied to international economic realities for much of the world's population. The two realms, that of economics and that of international politics, sat unhappily together in those years. It was never clear what their relative importance was, nor what their role was in shaping events. If talks between Mr Gorbachev and President Reagan offered some prospect of a safer world, was this necessarily a better world? The growing awareness of the need to tackle economic difficulties suggested that the political aspect of international relations was gradually being subordinated to the economic. The idea of independent state economies had therefore to give way to interdependence. The proposition was not new. Indeed, the origin of the concept of an international political economy had its roots in the sixteenth century, and had been finely developed in the nineteenth. But somehow the state had retained a pre-eminence. Governments kept a hold on currency values, not absolute it was true, but certainly relative, and their role was greater than that of any other single institution in the case of the major trading states. Many devices remained at the disposal of governments intent on protecting and enhancing their trade and production. The disappearance of the once almost ubiquitous Volkswagen 'Beetle', rear-engined motor car, was largely due to the political intervention of the government of the United States and its support for those who argued that the vehicle was unhealthy and unsafe. The legislation that followed eliminated the car from the roads of the USA within a few years in the 1970s, and for a brief period protected the home industry. It was no easy matter to smash the power of the state in economic policy.

But alongside this reality was the growing awareness of how many economic ties bound peoples together across national frontiers. Any doubt about this altogether more serious reality in international relations was dispelled by the impact of the fourfold rise in the price of oil in 1973 and in the following years. The question was not whether there was international interdependence, but how far that interdependence extended. The erosion of the international role of the state which interdependence implied, had both a political and an economic side. The crushing sense of international interdependence had grown since 1945. All governments were made aware that they did not make policy and war in isolation. By the time the USSR had developed nuclear weapons in 1949, all states were caught in the balance of power between the Soviet Union and the USA. The immediate impact was political. Foreign policy was not made in a vacuum with only local significance. No decision or action could be taken without drawing the attention of Moscow and Washington. No government could permit events to develop untempered by the attention of other states as they had in the 1930s. But economic interdependence introduced constraints on the role of government. These had a direct effect on the making of policy, comparable to constraints on the making of an independent foreign policy.

In the period after 1945, the awareness of an international dimension had been slow to evolve in the planning of economies and in trade. The consciousness of a truly international economy came with the creation of new institutions. The monetary system of the major states of the industrial world was realigned at the Bretton Woods conference in 1944, and lasted for almost thirty years. New economic agencies were established under the authority of the United Nations, stressing their international and political importance. The International Monetary Fund and the Bank for Reconstruction and Development were among the more significant in bringing governments together. In this way actual institutions for the management of the international economy were established. However, the success of the institutions was less certain. The importance of the agreements was perceived only gradually, although the increase in the number of new states encouraged the working of international economic contacts. These states needed help. Moreover, decolonisation accelerated the process. The former colonies often brought the assumption that the industrially developed states owed some kind of economic debt to the new states. There was no need to pose as Marxist in order to adopt the argument that former colonies should receive a proportion of the wealth that had been acquired by the erstwhile 'mother countries.' That usually also required the introduction of good management and stable politics.

The idea of economic interdependence developed rapidly in the 1970s. The stability of the currency system since the Bretton Woods agreement was rocked in 1971. New values were set in the Smithsonian agreements of December 1971 and these effectively ended the exchange system based on gold. By 1973 all the principal currencies were floating on the exchange markets. This general flotation suggested the collapse of economic interdependence, and a re-assertion of the role of government and sovereignty over the economy. But they actually introduced a carefully nurtured exchange market, with rules and quickly established traditions. Future government cooperation was invited and continued into the 1980s with discussion of currency values. However these arrangements were overtaken by the rise in oil prices in 1973. No other event had so shaken the idea of sovereignty over the economy. The sharp increase in the price of oil which followed the war between Israel and the Arab states threatened a widespread and serious recession. The continuing increases between 1974 and 1978 sustained the menace of economic catastrophe which neither completely materialised nor disappeared. The further sharp increase which followed the overthrow of the Shah's regime in Iran maintained this pressure. Between 1978 and 1980 a large price increase occurred, carrying the price to beyond $40 per barrel.

The perception of economic interdependence brought demands for new policies. In the 1980s interdependence became an accepted aspect of international relations.

Sovereignty was significantly eroded in economic matters—labour and employment, currency values. Although some of the inter-governmental institutions for the coordination of economic policies were not successful (e.g. the early attempts to create a Latin American Free-Trade Association), others moved towards economic integration. Certainly this occurred in Western Europe, but also among the ASEAN group of states in the Pacific, and in the Caribbean basin where the USA, the World Bank and local governments cooperated to promote stronger growth. The superpowers were sucked into the new world of interdependence. In the case of the USSR this was more by accident than in principle. The Soviet Union was no longer able to isolate its economy, but was drawn into the round of price increases and the impact of market forces. This was the result of greater trade with the free-market states. In addition, the East European socialist states became important suppliers of primary materials, and also of other goods. The economies of COMECON states became accustomed to price increases approximately in line with those in the rest of the world, and energy costs in the East rose accordingly. Moreover, the closed economic systems required free-market pricing in order to indicate values of goods. With no internal market pricing, it was theoretically impossible, and difficult in practice, to know what the relative cost was of tractors, lorries, railway rolling-stock and machinery. As inflation soared in the western economies, the East European states were obliged to take notice.

The United States had also seen prices and the value of the dollar adversely affected by events beyond the control of Washington. The impact of the American economy was always direct and immediate. Oil was priced in dollars. By 1978 the markets were set for a new larger increase in price, that took oil to $38 a barrel and sustained the momentum started five years earlier. But the real impact of the oil price rise was seen in the force of example. Other commodity producers followed the lead. They put up prices and they formed cartels with established institutions just as the oil producers had. The model of OPEC was followed by the producers of materials as diverse as bauxite and magnesium, jute and cotton. But the purpose was only partly economic and concerned with pricing and production. It was also political as was the purpose behind the oil price increases. International relations in the 1980s were very significantly to do with commodity agreements and the international redistribution of wealth.

New principles began to dominate international discourse. Consumer demand and production levels needed coordination. A just price had to be found. The 1970s gave the world a new dimension of politics, the North–South dialogue, preoccupied with the distribution of resources and riches and the need to create development where this had not existed. By the time President Reagan took office, the United States was committed to a programme of reconstruction. The new President went to the conference held at Cancún in Mexico, in October 1981. This had the inspiring title of the International Conference on Cooperation and Development. But the 1980s were a disappointment. The evolution of international relations revealed only the strength of the nation-state and the primacy of politics over economics, of international political relations over economic interdependence.

The years from 1980 to 1985 demonstrated the weakness of the assumptions behind economic interdependence, and the limited scope of the institutions that had been created for its expression. Older forces in international relations were shown to be more resilient. In the first place the USA proved more powerful and self-sufficient an economy than the events of 1971 and 1973 had suggested. Then the government in Washington was affected by the misery of the long-drawn-out war in Vietnam which had brought the most serious inflation since 1945. Watergate and the resignation of President Nixon followed. By 1980 and 1981, these events were put into a different perspective. Disengagement from the war and the stability of a political system that could expose and force such a revelation and such a resignation were regarded as strengths. The Reagan administration looked for and found a strong dollar. The relatively more significant drop in the international value of the currency in 1985 did not generally affect the underlying strength of the dollar during these years. Behind this strength were both the fact that the primary resources of the world were priced in dollars, and the continuing demonstration of the healthy economy of the USA. Almost to the surprise of the administration, production remained high, inflation fell and even unemployment figures improved. The new and rapidly expanding industries concerned with electronics and miniaturisation for computer production were successful, successfully competing with Japanese and West European production. A steady increase in industrial production in 1981 and 1982 turned into a sharp increase in 1983 and 1984. Interest rates dipped accordingly and although money was rather cheaper in Japan and the Federal Republic of Germany in the crucial years of 1983 and 1984, the USA remained the place to be for most businesses. The drift into a balance of trade deficit was serious and had consequences for international economic interdependence of another kind to which government paid increasing attention. But the essential element for the 1980s was the still great economic role played by the United States. Indeed the most rapidly expanding area of imported commodities was that of the Third World.

While imports from Europe into the USA fell steadily after 1978, those from Japan and Third World states rose, and the last category accounted for the largest share of US imports in 1982, outstripping those from Japan.[1] There was little doubt that the United States and its principal allies still possessed the economies to be reckoned with in the 1980s.

Moreover, the drive towards interdependence was also shaken by the fate of commodity prices. The role of oil and the political clout of the major oil-producing states did not develop as had been expected in the aftermath of the first large price increase in 1973. The price of oil began to fall. From the high point of $40 per barrel, the price collapsed. In the Autumn of 1985 the figure was below $20 and fell to below $10 for some grades of oil, stabilising at around $13 a barrel. In June 1982 the government of Mexico had undercut the agreed OPEC price, by asking only $30.6. There was no longer a broad agreement among the producing states. Other governments unilaterally moved out of line, like Nigeria and Iran. New production had commenced in several states, most notably the North Sea fields tapped by the United Kingdom and Norway, and the expansion of Alaskan production. The oil production from the Middle East had fallen from *c.*62 per cent of the main world production in 1973 to 40 per cent in 1983. Latin

American and Soviet production had increased, benefiting from the early price bonanza which followed 1973. These changes in production dampened the hopes of those who looked for new international economic order. There was no irreversible trend towards greater interdependence; governments retained many options. The institutions which were responsible for handling the pricing and production of oil also changed in the 1980s. The role of OPEC declined; producer and consumer states could not determine price or production. Even the place of the oil companies, once so vital and determining, had changed. The traders, quick-witted middle men, increasingly controlled the still vast dealings in oil. The centre of this market was London, and in 1983 handled oil valued at $275,000 million, 20 per cent of all international trade, and three times the annual budget of a state the size of France. This left oil as the world's most traded commodity, but the developments of that trade had less political importance than had been implied in 1973. By 1985 this change had been made quite clear, and the growing hold of the traders indicated this.

In addition, although oil consumption remained high, demand declined among the leading western industrial states. The pattern was not uniform, but the demand for oil in the years 1980–85 was in decline among those states relative to other sources of energy. The International Energy Agency showed the important growth in demand for coal, nuclear energy and natural gas.[2] Moreover, it was in the USA that the demand for oil declined most consistently; by 1983, there was an increase in demand in Western Europe and the fast developing economies of the Pacific—Japan, South Korea, Taiwan and Indonesia—which had increased its own oil production. The Middle East production suffered most in these years. The Iran–Iraq war caused a drop in the exports from those states and the Gulf states in general. Kuwait had a budget deficit in 1985. Thus the overall dependence of NATO states on oil from the Gulf had dropped from 31 per cent in 1979 to 13 per cent in 1983.[3] The scale of North American (i.e. USA and Canada) dependence declined from 13 to 3 per cent during the same years. Sources of supply had varied. The European states imported more than three times as much from

Latin America in 1983 as they had done in 1973. Their imports from the USSR doubled in the same decade.[4] The USA imported twice as much from Indonesia in 1983 as in 1973. But the policy of restraint and the diversification of supplies damaged the traditional producers. The emergence of the spot market after 1979 almost destroyed fixed price contracts. The scramble for better prices became more frantic as the cost per barrel fell below the $23 of the summer 1979, and the grip of the largest producer had slipped. The Saudia Arabian government had bowed to the pre-eminence of the traders. Oil was no longer a political weapon in international relations, but had being tamed by the market practices of the industrial states. The original price rise in 1973 had been in large measure related to the politics of the Middle East. One of the major intentions had been to bring changes of policy on the part of several governments towards Israel and the political future of the Palestinians. The political goal had been partly achieved, but since then the leverage was weaker.

Much the same trends had affected the producers of other vital primary commodities. Price increases and cooperation in pricing and production had been broadly modelled on the experience of the oil producers. The aim was a better deal for producing states and a redistribution of wealth. Primary commodity prices dropped with the fall in the price of oil. Alternative supplies and suppliers appeared. More effort was made to find substitutes and to reduce consumption. Above all the export of primary commodities from Latin American states increased to markets in the USA and Europe. Even such rare items as vanadium, required particularly in the manufacture of jet engines, were bought from new suppliers. The Republic of South Africa did not have a monopoly of such minerals. Peru re-entered the market, and competed with the mines of Namibia, and other southern African sources, for the large United States demand. The possibility of a single supplier exerting a hold on the market was less likely. The fall in prices not only affected minerals, but also vegetable produce—rubber, cacoa, jute, sugar, coffee—and many other basic products on the export of which several states depended. The recent peak in prices was reached in 1977, but since then the real price of the major primary products has almost halved, to stabilise at about 80 per cent of the 1975 level by 1984–5.[5] It was therefore difficult to see that the international order had changed very much in the 1980s. Governments and the market determined the development of the international economy.

Furthermore the creation of a new spirit of international cooperation and new institutions to give structure to an international economic order looked less than satisfactory by the 1980s. The basis had been laid in the blossoming North–South dialogue, encouraged by many politicians after the shock of the 1973 oil price rise. Trade at reasonable prices was not the only aim. Development of backward economies was also intended. The advantage was to be mutual. The geese that laid the golden eggs in the USA, Japan and Western Europe were not to be slaughtered, but nurtured so that the poorer states might benefit. The United States still held the greatest responsibilities. President Reagan did not disguise his belief in the competitive nature of the world economy, part of the contest between rival systems. On 29 September 1981, he spoke of the union of individual effort and economic reward through the 'magic of the market-place'.[6] But, before introducing his stringent domestic policies for the USA, affecting economy and budget, the President noted that this broader international ideal did not mean fatalism and the abandonment of the weakest. On the contrary, the policy required a programme for growth in the world economy and a policy to include 'all countries, especially the poorest ones', in this quest for growth and development. The first steps in this direction had already been taken. There had been two major developments towards the realisation of economic interdependence. The first had been an increasing degree of functional integration, the interlocking of economies through *ad hoc* arrangements. These carried a sense of inevitable interdependence, linking consumer and producer. They were given a degree of real permanence by the creation of special institutions, often concerned with particular commodities. The second development was a more general attempt to drive forward in unison, rich and poor states, states in all stages of development, states with different social systems. The drip by drip functional integration was not fast. New procedures were required to bring a more equitable market-place for the benefit of all. The groundwork for this had also started before President Reagan came into office.

In October 1981, President Reagan set out on one of his rare overseas journeys and went to Cancún in Mexico for the International Meeting on Cooperation and Development. This gathering, essentially in the spirit of the earlier Brandt Report on North–South cooperation, was concerned 'to focus on specific questions of substance, not on procedural matters'.[7]

The expected new international economic order was the guiding principle for the many meetings and agreements that followed. But the new system did not materialise. In the years 1981–85, the development of North–South dialogue was slow. No new principles were found on which the relations between industrial states, those in process of industrialisation and those producing primary commodities, might be based. The basis of economic relations between states was essentially unchanged. They all responded to market forces and to issues which sprang before them in a piecemeal way. Despite the tremendous optimism which created the Cancún conference, the international economy remained fixed in its traditional mould.

The commodity agreements were very limited in scope and failed to break into new and imaginative ground. The divisions among the oil producers had principally helped the industrialised states. But the haphazard stringing together of agreements on quota, price and production, in different commodities, meant that discussion of overall principles was neglected. The market for rubber was restructured in an agreement between the 33 states, both consumers and producers, which came into force in April 1982. However the fall in demand could not prevent a steady fall in price, and this agreement bore neither much relation to market forces nor to any general principles of North–South cooperation by 1985. Another agreement signed in 1982 covered the jute market, sensitive to growing competition from synthetic materials. Prospects for the success of this agreement seemed brighter. They were not for many other products, including sugar and some woods. In the case of the 1984 cacao agreement, neither the largest consumer, USA, nor the largest producer, the Ivory Coast, participated. Thus the prospects for a 'new international economic order' receded during the 1980s.

The saddest fate befell a grand scheme, that of the United Nations Conference on Trade and Development. This conference was created in 1964, on the initiative of the Third World states and the industrial states of Eastern Europe, but had developed more impetus with the enthusiasm for North–South dialogue in the 1970s. The full conference met, in principle, every four years, most recently at Belgrade in 1983. The previous full sessions had been held in Manila (1979), Nairobi (1976), Santiago (1972), New Delhi (1968) and the first at Geneva, the Mecca of many international illusions, in 1964. The aim was the creation of the 'new international economic order'. In a fine, acid, sentence, one commentator observed that the UNCTAD achievements were disapponting: 'the turgid and all but incomprehensible language of the UNCTAD resolutions, the haggling for small advantage, and the ubiquitous bureaucratic ambitions of UNCTAD seemed to suck the very life out of the endeavour'.[8] The achievements of UNCTAD were disappointing. Only one agreement was reached which incorporated a price stabilisation mechanism, the stock reserve applying to the international rubber market. Although the original group of 77 had become over 120 by the 1980s, a leading economist, Professor I.M.D. Little, assessed the gains for the South as a result of their solidarity as minimal.[9] Paradoxically, he argued that 'pressure in non-UNCTAD assemblies . . . has been more successful'.[10] The great disparities in wealth and requirements among the countries of the South was partly responsible for the negative result. The differences were considerable. The leading producer states, whether of oil or other essential materials like bauxite or copper, had benefited during the years of high prices. These had occurred in the mid-1970s. Their strength had cushioned them when prices fell with the ever-nagging fear of recession. They had also managed to diversify and slowly attempt to build new wealth-creating industries. At the other extreme were states with few usable resources in the short term. Some, like Chad, had to face war. Others faced drought and famine. The terrible cost to states like Ethiopia and Sudan could scarcely be tackled and met in the meetings of UNCTAD.

In the Pacific basin particularly there were states which had managed to build important and very competitive industries, selling into the markets of the European and North American states. Such a spread of interests led too easily to banal demands and all too often to confrontation, as most studies of the contemporary institutions of the international order have revealed.

A further limitation had been the ambiguous role of the USSR and those states associated with its economy and economic institutions. These states could provide neither the markets nor the reliable supply of goods required by many developing economies. Into the 1980s even socialist economies, and governments politically closer in attitude to the Soviet Union, were still looking to West European, North American or Japanese companies for aid and practical assistance. The examples of Angola and Mozambique were among the more notable in these years. Several western and Soviet bloc technicians and specialists worked there. In some cases the Soviet Union and COMECON partners boldly bought raw materials in order to protect the fragile socialist economies. The example of Cuban sugar purchases was among the oldest of these, but Nicaraguan coffee and bananas were treated in a similar way after 1980. However the economic strength of the industrial economies of the USA, Japan and some European states shifted the political balance in favour of the free-market states on whom the total prosperity depended. There had been a complete reversal of emphasis by 1985, away from the initiative held by the key primary producing states, like the members of OPEC, to the United States and those other states which had avoided recession, kept up employment and currency values, and also moved into the new industrial manufacturing of electronic equipment and lasers and automated factory production.

Some international agreements avoided the generalities, the confrontation and the ultimate inertia of UNCTAD. Some were very local and bilateral arrangements, often made between developing states and a former colonial power, as those beneficial contracts negotiated through the British Overseas Development Institute. Other agreements were wider in application and among these the conventions of the European Community for African, Caribbean and Pacific states were increasingly important. The value of these conventions, originally the Yaoundé convention but then three Lomé conventions, lay in the preferential trade terms and associated aid which linked the industrial European economies to the Third World countries. Although the majority of early signatories were former French colonies, the convention was rapidly widened, especially after the entry of the United Kingdom into the European Community. Former Commonwealth Preference arrangements were incorporated into the Lomé negotations. Moreover these agreements concerned the import of manufactured goods from participating African, Caribbean and Pacific states into the European Community which were permitted without restrictive quotas. The development of diverse industry was therefore encouraged by such arrangements. Nevertheless, the very success of the Lomé style of international cooperation across the North–South divide hampered any more comprehensive international economic system. Not only were other Third World states excluded, but also the advantages of this trade came only to the European Community states and not, for example, to the USA or Japan. In addition, the economic benefits for participants exacerbated differences in wealth among the states of the South. The success of these agreements further impeded the overall North–South dialogue and the UNCTAD efforts.

The failure to create genuine economic interdependence as opposed to haphazard commodity dependence and mutually beneficial trade, led to the most significant fact of international relations in the 1980s, the strength of the economy of the USA. Disparities in economic performance did not really diminish and the United States held on to its important role among developed industrial economies. One of the puzzles of the years 1981–86 was the relative success of the economic performance of the United States. This was almost achieved despite the policies of the government. Taxes were cut, but spending was not reduced. By the second term of the Reagan administration it seemed that the economy was being 'pumped' by the sustained spending on defence, and the budget deficit worsened. However, simultaneously the USA experienced reductions in unemployment figures, generally more successful than those of West European partners and competitors. Inflation was also reduced, from 12 per cent in 1981 to *c*.3 per cent in 1985. High interest rates, government borrowing and a nagging deficit notwithstanding, commercial prospects in the United States remained good and confidence bouyant during this period.

The unexpected nature of this performance by the United States made the trend more significant. Hopes were boosted and the leadership of the USA was all the more readily accepted in the other capitals of the industrial, free-market states. Thus the United States was able to persuade those governments to participate in an occasional and coordinated intervention in the currency markets at the summit meeting in Versailles in 1982, thereby controlling wild fluctuation of values and assisting the growth that the government of the United States wished to promote and sustain. But success meant that disparities did not vanish; they barely even declined in the years 1980–85. This had a general significance, that the traditionally strongest economies remained so. There was also a more confusing pattern of economic success and international dependence. Some of the worst aspects of the latter came with serious accumulations of debt. This affected some East European states but most severely the impoverished economies of some Latin American states. Mexico and Brazil were among the worst cases of debt in the 1980s, essentially middle-income states which appeared to offer some credit for international public and private loans. In these cases, the optimism was misplaced although changes of government, like that in Brazil in 1985, suggested an improved prospect. The world's poorest states could not offer the credit to attract equivalent amounts of loan, and thus states like Lesotho and Chad had much less serious debt problems. However the growing disparities left states like the USA in an ever more powerful position in the international economy. Even those states which had experienced a degree of economic boom, such as Taiwan and South Korea, traded increasingly with the United States. Indeed in the 1980s, the Pacific area was the fastest expanding area for American trade. The USA had replaced much of its trade with Europe with trade with Asian states and with Third World producers of manufactured, semi-manufactured goods as well as primary materials.[11]

The burden of international economic regulation therefore remained with the industrial and developed states in the 1980s. They persisted in their efforts to further free trade, through the negotiating rounds of the General Agreement on Tariffs and Trade and through the economic summit meetings of their economic leaders. Such meetings were held regularly; the first attended by President Reagan was at Ottawa, in October 1981. The principles were clear and firm, freer trade, assistance for the less developed states, low inflation and stable monetary growth, lower debts and lower unemployment. But within the statement of these aims was the not entirely consistent declaration of intent that hinted at protection. At Ottawa, in the final Declaration, dated 21 July 1981, the notion was clear: 'The primary challenge we addressed at this meeting was the need to revitalise the economies of the industrial democracies, to meet the needs of our own people and strengthen world prosperity'.[12] The lesson of the previous decade had been that it was essential to put one's own house in order first. The trend of the years 1981–85 was therefore towards the assertion of economic nationalism and protectionism.

The trend was never direct and clear. Great efforts were made to prevent a return to an old-fashioned protectionism. Discussions between the industrial economies were particularly devoted to this aim. The opening of Japanese markets to more manufactured goods from the USA and Western Europe was an important element in this effort to keep markets free. The goal was not easily attained or even perceived. Businessmen and parliamentary representatives were nervous about hastily made concessions. They wished to support those industries in danger of collapse before sharp foreign competition and to maintain levels of employment which were falling in all western states. In many cases the governments were obliged to adhere to the more open goals of the meetings between the industrial leaders. Mrs Thatcher and President Reagan were joined in their ideals of freer trade by the leaders of Japan and the rest of the European Community states. The pressure for some element of economic nationalism was never far away once they returned to their Cabinets and Parliaments. Congress was nervous of renewed inflation, job losses and fierce competition in all manner of goods from motor cars to computers and electronic goods. The Japanese remained able to restrict entry of many goods by quotas and other devices. Above all the continuing application of non-tariff barriers eluded proper and agreed international control. Quotas and other types of non-tariff barrier, perhaps most especially the application of special standards to performance and quality of imports thus protecting the domestic products, were not new. However there seemed to be general agreement that they only became more significant in the mid-1970s. The established free trade organisations, e.g. the GATT negotiations, failed to grapple with these powerful devices for the exercise of economic nationalism.[13] Some of the restrictions were very effective, limiting the size of driving mirrors, the length of windscreen wipers, the test hours for multi-transistor chips, the lead emission of car fuel—the list seemed endless and few states were innocent of the application of such devices which were notionally prohibited by international agreement among the members of GATT.

Several of the tenser relations between the USA and the European Community concerned economic protection. The associated and other agreements between the Community and non-member states worked to the apparent disadvantage of the USA. Thus the Lomé states were drawn into closer trading relationship with the European Community than with the USA, and in the case of the Caribbean threatened to reverse the earlier trend which had pulled them into a closer trading partnership with the USA.[14] Agricultural trading policy had long been a cause of dispute between the Community and the United States. The latter regarded the Common Agricultural Policy and the pricing system as protectionist; US surplus production could not readily enter the Common Market area and compete with the European output. There were other sectors of industry that experienced a return to protectionism. Resentment was felt in the USA over European competition and market controls for steel in the early 1980s. Serious unemployment affected both European and American steel towns—Corby as much as Bethlehem, Pennsylvannia. The

United States had 'become uncompetitive with other countries that we helped to rebuild in the Marshall plan and who now have more modern facilities than we do'.[15] However, these tensions did not impinge on foreign policy agreements any more than United States pressure to stop the gas pipeline contracts exposed fundamental differences of view between the USA and the European allies. In both cases, economic interests were adjusted to national not international needs, but the principles of foreign policy were less directly affected. A short-lived disagreement proved almost irrelevant to NATO strategy and western strategic interests in general. There was really no contradiction between the assertion of national economic interests and the appeal for a foreign policy based on the principle of freedom. The economic goals set by the Reagan administration were those of market forces linked to freedom of choice. But these market forces were those of the economist Milton Friedman, not the forces of chaos but of a carefully regulated and nurtured market. The very word 'market' implied attention to free competition and the creation of a structure in which it might operate. The most important institution was therefore the nation-state.

Interdependence foundered on the resilience of the state. Its interests were paramount. Even the largest of international companies accepted the terms laid down by governments and adjusted their trading accordingly. The relative size of economic holdings was irrelevant. Although great corporations, trading in many states, had incomes and investments larger than many individual states, none of them made laws, participated in agreements to which only governments were parties, and possessed the range of obligations and facilities available to governments. Oil companies could negotiate and were of great importance to oil-producing states, but the governments retained a significant initiative, in determining prices and quotas, in making war and peace. Few political leaders have been so forthright in asserting the primacy of government in international economic matters as the President of Peru, Alan Garcia, elected in 1985. Although Peru owed some $600 millions, the Social-Democratic leader was defiant. His government nationalised three major international companies' assets in Peru, and recommended negotiations on their future trading. He told the journalists assembled at Punta-del-Este in Uruguay in February 1986 for the meeting of heavily indebted Latin American states, that although the governments belonged to the International Monetary Fund, 'we cannot accept that it pulls the strings as if we were puppets, and that it subjects us to a currency, the dollar'.[16]

The international economic order was firmly subordinated to the politics of international relations. In these issues the USA was still the most important government, just as it had been in 1945. The blemishes on American power had been obliterated and the participation of the government of the United States was both required and criticised in the 1980s by those governments hoping for more stability and economic improvement. The USA remained the largest contributor of aid in the world. For the drought and famine-affected states of Africa, the USA provided more relief, in materials and in personnel, than any other government, and more than the much publicised Band Aid charity programme. The Third World, whether developing or less developed, depended on western assistance and that meant the primacy of the state in its traditional form.

The USSR was not excluded from the world economy, but the system was maintained as a protective economy. New states participated in COMECON arrangements which had ceased to be an Eastern European closed system. The Soviet Union traded more widely, provided advisers and specialists, and bought into commodity markets on a scale unknown in earlier decades. Many crucial primary products were only available from the Soviet Union and a few other states like the Republic of South Africa, Angola or Zaire. This applied especially to some minerals, including bauxite, gold, chrome ore and manganese ores. Thus there were significant changes in the pattern of Soviet foreign trade in the 1980s. In the previous decade, trade with the West European states and OECD states in general had been the fastest expanding sector, but this was no longer the case. Socialist countries were increasing their trade faster than OECD members by 1984.[17] Soviet trade with developing states also expanded faster than that with OECD states in the 1980s. This trade had amounted to an estimated 13 per cent of Soviet external trade in 1984.[18] Moreover, according to one analyst, Soviet trade with the Third World was increasingly conducted on the barter or 'clearing' principle, the exchange of goods.[19] Thus in exchange for Indian tea and jute, the USSR might trade arms. In many ways arms sales and the building of weapons factories were among the more successful Soviet and East European exports. For many developing states, the purchase of Soviet arms was not regarded as incompatible with both a degree of socialism and contracts with major American and European companies. Gulf Oil company activity, Soviet arms and a kind of progressive socialist ideology thus characterised Angola in the 1980s.

The market for arms was expanding in the Third World and ripe for Soviet and other government contracts. Some European defence budgets declined between 1980 and 1985, but most states outside Europe increased their expenditure. In the case of the Middle East, the increases approached a doubling of the military budgets.[20] The overall increases meant important markets for all the main suppliers, whether these were direct sales, credit arrangements or equipment grants. The variety of particular deals made accurate estimates difficult to achieve. Some indication of the expansion and value of the arms market was given in the figures for French arms exports under the socialist government of the 1980s. In 1982, there was as much as a 23 per cent growth over the previous year; the total value in 1982 was 41,600 million francs. The increase of purchases in the Middle East and North Africa was 65 per cent.[21] In 1983 the government of Iraq bought up to sixty Mirage F-1 aircraft and Exocet missiles from France, further increasing their share of French military exports. In the 1980s, the Soviet Union was not only exporting but had organised the manufacture of small arms and other weapons in several countries in the Middle East, and supplied tanks and aircraft to many states.

Other factors also boosted the arms market. Technical developments meant earlier obsolescence. This was not only a matter of electronic and laser technology, but also basic mechanical components. The ability of artillery and tank weapons to hit targets was dependent on more and more accurate new techniques. However the changes in the design of vehicle suspension were as significant, and failure to compete meant that older designs were slower, less capable of firing accurately while on the move, and more tiring to operate. By 1985 some of the most interesting innovations lay in the design of tracked vehicle suspension units. Therefore into the 1980s, the arms industries were providing a world-wide increase in the most technically complex weapons and equipment as well as the more basic but effective items like Soviet-designed machine and automatic guns.

The major manufacturers remained the Soviet Union, USA and France, but some changes had occurred in the 1980s. Important European arms manufacturing states continued to meet both domestic needs and to participate in cooperative projects. This was particularly the case among the NATO allies. A state like the Federal Republic of Germany was engaged in a great range of cooperative projects with the United Kingdom (missile systems, howitzers, aircraft, frigates and artillery systems), France (reconnaissance systems, helicopters, artillery and anti-tank rockets and missiles), Italy (aircraft and frigates) and the USA (defence missiles, and various naval and artillery defence systems).[22] However the defence element in the West German industrial production was still very small, on average less than 4 per cent of the total value produced.[23] The defence element was largest in the aircraft industry, and in the munitions and weapons industries where the percentage was over 50 per cent. The significant expansion of arms industries with a potential for export, came from states which had no tradition of established industries. The Republic of South Africa produced increasing quantities of weapons and defence-related equipment. More important was the expansion of the industry in other states, including less developed economies. Thus by 1985, Brazil was one of the foremost armament manufacturing states. In particular, Brazil produced tracked and other military vehicles, often buying or collaborating with European manufacturers like Mercedes-Benz (for engines) and British suppliers. The world's most sophisticated tank chassis and suspension unit was being developed in Brazil by 1985. Indeed the arms industry had the possibility of becoming one of the most effective motors for economic growth.

International economic goals were not reached through a successful progress towards interdependence. After so much enthusiasm for international cooperation and the active participation in new institutions, much of this drive had faded in the years 1980–85. Above all no principles were agreed for the redistribution of wealth and the promotion of growth. The more successful achievements were the result of *ad hoc* agreements and careful inter-government negotiations. Firm and stable government therefore offered the best prospect of economic improvement. When President Garcia nationalised foreign assets and refused to clear the arrears on Peruvian international debt, he also presented a fresh political stability and the chance to renegotiate the terms of these economic ties. The vaunted economic interdependence had not resulted in an erosion of state sovereignty; it had given it a new importance. Wherever aid or economic assistance and the encouragement of commerce was required, the state and its efficient administration were paramount, as they had been for centuries. Even so dramatic a relief scheme as that which poured help into Ethiopia in 1984 and 1985 was ultimately dependent upon how the government of the state handled the operations, what security and facilities were offered, and how effectively those offers were carried out. International economic institutions therefore were essentially a means of bringing states and their governments together, not for the erosion of sovereignty and the opening of a new era of interdependence.

If states were still strong and the moral ascendancy of the South had not been transformed into a new equality, two states were still more important than all the rest, the Soviet Union and the United States. However the USA stood out among these states as the most important creditor for many governments. Although the United States were not always the most substantial trading partner, no government could ignore the policies of the USA. The attitude of the government in Washington was still the single most significant factor in the international political economy. Moreover under the Reagan administration the United States economy stayed strong. The great home market of the United States and Canada and the strength of the currency were the basis of this buoyancy in the 1980s. Government policies may have contributed to the apparently boundless energy of the country. New areas became booming and prosperous development zones. Such were Arizona, the 'Waterbelt' of the Great Lakes, and above all 'Automation Valley' was 'tipped' as the profitable area for 1986. Only a few of the states of the Far East matched the constant productivity of the United States.

But the important role of the USA in the international economy and the weakness of any truly interdependent institutions, served to reinforce the classical elements in international relations. While such exciting and obviously successful private ventures to bind the economies and efforts of nations together as that of aid programmes for African famine in 1985 and 1986 cut across state frontiers, the major emphasis lay with governments. Even the United Nations failed to bring interdependence. Political control of economic policy was exercised by sovereign governments, and was obliged to accept the validity of frontiers. However the failure to settle political disputes at the supra-state level left the economies exposed to the political requirements of the state. Nothing had changed. The Secretary General of the United Nations, Mr Perez de Cuellar, attempted to achieve greater international harmony and open more doors for economic cooperation, but this gentle and industrious Peruvian who travelled with the vigour of Dr Kissinger in pursuit of order, failed to establish firm principles for international political economy. The USA in particular had no new reason for trusting international organisations devoted to the redistribution of wealth. They were often dependent on American money, but incapable of stopping corruption and waste. In 1984, the government of the United States withdrew from UNESCO.

International economic cooperation remained *ad hoc* and dependent on the will of government. National sovereignty was not eroded. There were few steps towards long-term functional integration. Liberal thought in the nineteenth century had expected international trade to bring harmony and peace. Minimal levels of cooperation in the 1980s had not brought interdependence nearer. The more successful events had been the purely coincidental, the operations for famine relief, and flood and other disasters had brought governments together. But the sharing of airstrips and coordination of supply dropping zones did not open the way to economic interdependence.

The avid and morally sound demands for a new international economic order had failed to penetrate the requirements of the state. However the relative failure of the North–South dialogue in the 1970s, did not mean a return to the East–West clash of political economies. There were new elements at work, already established by the start of the decade in 1980. The first was the continued primacy of the USA in the international economy. The politics of the United States had not been reduced to subservience by the pressure of oil and other price rises. Politics and economics were resilient in the long run, almost to the surprise of some members of the Reagan administration. In addition there were new areas of economic growth to which the international community had to respond. These were essentially in the Pacific and the Far East. Economic prosperity and growth there, gave greater importance to the political future of the region.[24]

A further feature of the newer economic order to emerge from the 1970s was the stress on arms and the armament industries as both necessary for the security of the state and as means of injecting some growth into the economy. This applied not merely to the United States, but yet more to many developing economies. The failure to create economic interdependence meant the continuity of state sovereignty, and stress on the autonomy of the state meant defence and war.

NOTES

1. Imports into the United States from Third World countries were valued at $163 milliard in 1983, i.e. 28 per cent of total US imports, *Le Monde,* quoting OECD sources, 5 June 1984.
2. *The Times,* 10 January 1986.
3. T. Cutler, 'NATO and oil supply vulnerability', *NATO Review,* October 1984, p. 31.

4. European oil imports from Latin America grew from 17.5 million tonnes in 1973 to 40.5 m tonnes in 1983. In 1983, the Soviet Union sold 87.8 million tonnes to European states outside the Soviet bloc. *Le Monde,* 29 January 1985.
5. United Nations Conference on Trade and Development, official statistics, 1985.
6. At the annual meeting of the Board of Governors of the World Bank and IMF, *Public Papers,* p. 854.
7. President Reagan, at the first plenary session, 22 October 1981, *Public Papers,* p. 982.
8. R.K. Olson, *United States Foreign Policy and the New International Economic Order, 1974–1981* (Pinter, New York, 1981), p. 62.
9. 'Has the South in fact gained anything of value as a result of solidarity and confrontation? The analysis of this book has proclaimed the answer to be "No" at least so far as trade is concerned'. I.M.D. Little, *Economic Development. Theory, policy and International relations* (Basic Books, New York, 1982), p. 383.
10. *Ibid.*
11. Imports from Europe had declined from being 43 per cent of United States' imports to 24 per cent in the period 1966–83. Cf. above p. 117 and *Le Monde* 5 June 1984.
12. *Public Papers,* p. 646.
13. Little, *op.cit.,* p. 302.
14. Caribbean trade was concentrated on North America rather than Europe. This also applied to Commonwealth states. For example Jamaican trade with the United Kingdom declined by 9 per cent over the years 1976–82, but trade with the USA expanded by 25 per cent in the same period. See United Nations, *International Trade Statistics* (1985).
15. Presidential press conference, 27 December 1981, *Public Papers,* p. 1196.
16. Press report, *Le Monde* 28 February 1986.
17. Trade with West Europe declined in the same period.
18. By 1984 the most important Soviet trading partners in the developing world were India, with Argentina and Libya rather further behind. D. Dhombres, 'USSR: l'arme du commerce exterieur', *Le Monde,* 'Economie', 26 March 1985.
19. *Ibid.,* p. 19.
20. Institute for Strategic Studies, defence budgets, 1985, *Military Balance* (IISS, London, 1985).
21. French defence survey, *Le Monde,* April 1983.
22. Defence *White Paper,* 1985, p. 364.
23. *Ibid.,* p. 367.
24. R. Holbrooke, 'East Asia: the next challenge', *Foreign Affairs,* Spring 1986, pp. 732-51.

5 Arms and War

The formidable nature of military resources held by the Soviet Union and the United States implied the survival of superpower influence into the last twenty years of the century. The range, quantity and innovative quality of their arsenals remained intimidating. But there was an element of illusion. While the superpowers discussed arms control and created and developed new strategic weapons and placed major investment in battlefield systems, other trends broke into their secure domination. Perhaps the superpower control had never been secure; the events of the years 1980–86 revealed further gaps in their influence.

The huge military power of the USA and of the Soviet Union bore an increasingly irrelevant appearance. War and political disruption spread in such a manner as to render this investment almost meaningless as a vehicle for international intervention. Attempts to prevent this happening were made. In particular the military versatility of the major states was improved. The concept of a highly mobile and substantial force for rapid intervention became more familiar. The USA already possessed a rapid deployment force. The USSR had explored more mobile warfare and spent heavily on helicopters, airborne troops and more modern equipment. The French government also looked into the possibility of a rapid action force.[1] But this stress on more flexible forces underlined the less predictable circumstances in which hostilities occurred.

Both the USA and the Soviet Union faced new forces in international relations. The cumulative effect of many changes was only felt round about 1980. The last decolonisations occurred between 1975 and 1980, those of the Portuguese territories in Africa and the negotiated independence of Zimbabwe. As the number of states increased, many of them fragile and unstable, so did the quantity of arms. This factor alone transformed international relations and the position of the superpowers. By the end of the 1970s, the impact of oil and other price increases, the threat of recession which nagged developed industrial countries, inflation in the USA after the war in Vietnam, all had altered the international distribution of wealth. Those states which obtained a relative increase in wealth were able to increase expenditure on arms or on the development of an armaments industry. Third World states became major exporters of weapons. In the 1980s Brazil exported to 28 other states, representing 80 per cent of its production.[2] Some production was manufactured under licence, like the Egyptian assembly of French Puma and Gazelle helicopters. In other cases, the conception and manufacture was totally indigenous, as with the Argentinian Pucara aircraft, the Brazilian Tucan aircraft, and a variety of ground and naval equipment made in South Korea. Even small states like Malaysia, Singapore and North Korea, were intent on big expansion programmes for armaments. Other states were already substantial producers for domestic and international demand, Israel, South Africa, Iran, India (with its own nuclear capability) and Taiwan. Third World arms sales were estimated to have reached $2000 million in 1984 according to the Stockholm Peace Research Institute.

The motivation, despite the great cost and lengthy development programmes required for quantity production of weapons, was the striving for some degree of self-sufficiency. Dependence upon outside military aid was risky, as Iran, Iraq and Argentina discovered between 1980 and 1986. Embargoes and temporary sanctions might easily be imposed, and this occurred in the cases of South Africa, Chile, Iran and the Argentine. Other motives also applied. The armament industry provided employment and the prospect of exports. In a state like Brazil, with a large industry, manufacturing tanks, aircraft, other armoured vehicles (the basic chassis was a Brazilian component, although guns, engines and suspension systems, and electronic equipment might be bought elsewhere, usually in Western Europe) and smaller infantry weapons, the economic benefit was necessarily important. In addition, as the potential for local war and threats of war grew, the need for governments to possess effective defence systems also grew. The state had to be defended, and that meant the growth in expenditure on arms and, where possible, the creation of defence industries. This was a phenomenon of world-wide proportions only in the 1980s. The effect on the United States and the Soviet Union was equally significant and decisive. The economic developments of the 1970s brought new purchasing potential to different states, those with oil and energy resources and those with big investment in new industries and new automated production techniques. Much of the wealth had gone into armaments.

The cost of war and guarding against war had grown vastly. The inflationary developments of the decade 1970–80 was partly responsible. New techniques were another reason for the increases. For the USA and the Soviet Union there were two costs. First, they had to arm against each other, the great costs of deterrence in its classical post-1945 form. Second, was that of arming in relation to other states and for the possibility of conflict, of less defined contingencies than war with each other. This second cost had also risen exceptionally during the 1970s. There were more states and more instability, and there were a greater variety of offensive and defensive systems available. In 1950, the USA and the USSR had overwhelming military strength. By 1980, the quantity of military equipment and the armed potential distributed around the world could scarcely be matched by either of the superpowers. The term 'superpower' had lost some of its meaning as a result. The governments in Washington and Moscow were more restricted in the scope of their foreign and defence policies. Only in nuclear weapons and the more sophisticated equipment, could the two superpowers claim to retain a commanding position.

The change in the relative military capability had been partly caused by the continual arming and re-arming of Soviet and American allies. Huge quantities of weapons had been made available, through loan and credit arrangements, through direct purchase and through military aid. The accumulation of this material and its spread among the growing number of states ultimately weakened the influential position of the United States and of the Soviet Union. A major military commitment in one area by either of them, affected their relative strength elsewhere. The cost of trying to maintain a global military capacity which also was a credible capacity, was not only enormous but almost impossible. The United States government obtained Congressional approval for a defence budget of $302,500,000,000 in October 1985. This was the budget for the fiscal year 1985–86[3] This great sum was principally concerned with the major defence commitments of the USA. All other states were increasing arms expenditure, with only a few exceptions. The diversity of equipment among so many states, made military planning immeasurably hard.

The imbalance that existed between different regions reflected the vagaries of international tensions. In the 1980s, the Near and Middle East continued to experience big increases in defence expenditure. This was less true for the Pacific but there the differences were great from one state to another. Only the North Koreans more than doubled defence expenditure between 1978 and 1984.[4] In the Near and Middle East most states more than doubled their expenditure between 1980 and 1985. Iraq was thought to have achieved an increase from $2 billion in 1980 to *c.*$14 billion in 1984. Much of this expenditure went on modern combat aircraft—American, Russian or French for the most part—and on helicopters and tanks. The ability of some states to wage war was seen to be remarkable. The Vietnamese had fought the Americans, the People's Republic of China and more than a decade after their victorious entry into Saigon, were still fighting in Kampuchea. The war between Iran and Iraq entered its sixth year in 1985.

Moreover the withdrawal of troops from Vietnam by the government of the USA and the cautious policies of the Soviet Union, meant that more states escaped superpower control and military influence. Some observers had noted that the Soviet Union had managed to take advantage of the reluctance of the government and Congress of the United States to authorise intervention after Vietnam. Soviet troops were clearly in Afghanistan, and their specialists, technicians and military advisers were active in a number of states, particularly in Africa. But there was no major Soviet military involvement apart from that in Afghanistan during the 1980s. Yet the continued supply, credit, gift or sales of all kinds of arms created a world of exceptionally well-armed governments, capable of sustaining serious and even prolonged warfare. The governments possessed modern missile defence systems, such that even American and Soviet aircraft were at risk from small states, and the mobile ground forces with air support capable of fighting destructive wars. The quantities of small arms and automatic weapons available in all the continents were adequate to provide the means of war for generations. In parts of North Africa, there had been a continuous supply of such equipment from the days of the German *Afrikakorps,* through the Algerian War, lasting from 1954 until 1962 and involving 500,000 French troops, into the decades of the Palestinian agitiation and the widespread manufacture of simple, tough and locally produced firearms. From Central America, across Africa and the East, the young—often the very young—and the old had the means of war. The governments of both the United States and the Soviet Union could only regard this development as beyond ready political control and, a characteristic of the 1980s, there was hardly any possibility of either state dominating such regions.

Soviet and United States influence was also restricted by the build-up in armed forces by several states. The size of armies increased, and this in turn limited the kind of military intervention that either of the erstwhile superpowers might contemplate with confidence. The USA had learned in Vietnam that very large numbers of troops were required to sustain a war. After the vicious Tet offensive in 1968, the American commanders wanted another 210,000 men to bring the United States forces up to almost 740,000. This request was refused by President Johnson's administration. But lengthy involvement anywhere would require large numbers of trained men. The limited Soviet action in Afghanistan, a war kept to confined areas and hardly a mobile war, required approximately 115,000 men by 1985. The size of many of the 'new armies' of the 1980s was proportionately great. By 1984, for example, the South Koreans had almost 600,000 troops, virtually twice the size of the British forces. Indonesia had 278,000 and Taiwan 440,000. The removal of American forces from South Korea had led the Japanese to increase their defence budgets. Although traditionally restricted after the Second World War and with a powerful pacifist lobby, the Japanese growth in military material and men was steady. In 1984 there were almost 250,000 in the regular units. The army possessed more than 1000 tanks, and the Japanese airforce had over 250 combat aircraft and 44,000 personnel.[5] While the European Defence Ministries urged greater spending and governments and NATO delegations strove for marginal increases which were not really sustained during the 1980s, the governments of Third World states and of the industrialised states of the Far East managed to produce constant expansion of military capacity. This had little to do with communist/ capitalist ideological divisions, but with the nature of the state and the assertion and insecurity of government. The availability of arms reached a scale which was completely unprecedented and disrupted the assumptions that had conditioned behaviour and judgements in international relations since 1945.

Two distinct effects were noted in the United States and, it would seem, in the Soviet Union. The first was the maintenance of military strength, indeed the increase in defence budgets. All aspects, new techniques, versatility in equipment and large-scale production, were sustained. The United States' defence expenditure still far exceeded that of western and Third World states. The second effect was to increase the need for a military capability that could intervene anywhere, in all manner of ways, in short to maximise military flexibility. This in turn meant that the United States, like the Soviet Union, was operating in a more divided and less secure international environment. Governments and policies were less interdependent.

War became more likely in principle as the world became further removed from the miserable stability which was the legacy of the Second World War. The principle which gave way in the years after 1945 was that of certain dependence, a dependence from which few states were exempt. The alignments formed during and immediately after the world war gave a distinct shape to international political relations. The commanding position of the victors and the subsequent ideological division between them, afforded some governments the opportunity and presented others with the necessity to draw close to one side or the other. Yet several factors destroyed the basis of this anxious but orderly condition.

The grand era of five or six major states with a ring of dependent territories whose governments had few decisions to make about foreign policy, vanished before 1939. The acceptability of empire was discredited during the war and the residue of colonies and protectorates was whittled away after 1945. However this took time, and was hardly completed until the later part of the 1960s, or even the following decade. The shattering of the early bonds which accompanied Cold War occurred long before the high point of détente in the era of Dr Kissinger's diplomacy. There were alternatives in foreign policy open to many governments as was demonstrated by the Bandung meeting of non-aligned states in 1955, by the experience of governments like those of Egypt (after the 1952 revolution), Morocco and Tunisia after independence, and Algeria after 1962. The same was shown by the vacillations of Cuban policy in the immediate aftermath of the successful Castro insurrection in 1959, before the firm association with the Soviet Union which followed in 1960. In this turmoil principles for the guidance of government in making policies were not easy to find. Subservience to imperial traditions and dictates had gone. The contemporary form of hegemony, often referred to as new imperialism, whether of Soviet or western inspiration, was not securely binding on the governments of new states. These were exposed to a genuine form of balance of power.

The demands of some ideological preference had to be balanced against the fear of oblivion, not caused by nuclear war but by domestic revolt or invasion and intervention from some neighbouring government. As the division of the world which had emerged after 1945 began to crumble and modify, the balance between these forces shifted in favour of the need to defend against the fear of destruction for the governments of many new states. The basis of policy became the need for comparison with other states in the immediate vicinity, were they more powerful or less? were their military and economic resources disproportionately large and therefore threatening to local stability and balance of power? These factors predisposed the governments of new states to seek security in military means. As superpower influence became less assertive and governments eluded their control, the propensity for war increased. This applied in regions with a long history of violence and even war, like South East Asia or the Middle East, and to regions where conflict had been more restricted, like Central America. In areas like the last, there were more options in the 1980s than before because not only Cuba but also Nicaragua had escaped the domination of the United States. Contiguous states like Honduras needed to maintain independence from the USA and also to seek effective competitive margins in order to face the military capacity of Nicaragua. The regional balance, competition and more states, meant war.

At the end of the Second World War less than fifty states participated in the newly formed United Nations. Although a rush of governments to sign the declaration and join the international organisation occurred almost immediately, the world of states remained small, compact and familiar. By 1980 the cluster of states had tripled. The 157 states were of very different economic capability and political stability. In 1945 size and tradition played a significant part in determining international importance. The great number of states, the virtual end of the process of decolonisation which had released many European colonies, confused the assessment of political importance in the 1980s. Some of the smallest states had great strategic and political significance. Tiny island republics in the oceans acquired a new role. With fewer domestic political complexities than some larger, land-locked state, many became vital military outposts for supply and signals observation. The Cape Verde islands served as a vital link between the Americas and Africa. Cuban aircraft used the facilities, and the civil airlines of the Republic of South Africa paid for landing and refuelling rights. Islands like Gan, Masira, Ascension, Diego Garcia, Réunion (not all were yet independent) had increasing importance, as did the Seychelles and Mauritius. The much larger political world of the 1980s did not make for stability and order.

International stability was not encouraged by the chronic poverty and constitutional instability of many of these states. The rush for independence and a seat at the United Nations Assemby in New York, did not disguise the fact that the existence of many of the member states was precarious. Natural obstacles to wealth were seriously disruptive. Drought affected most of central and northern Africa in the 1980s, as it did southern Europe, and political strains were the inevitable result. War in Ethiopia and Somalia, ostensibly over the area known as Ogaden, with the few meagre waterways flowing down from the hills around Jijiga, was one such conflict. There were many others, in Mali and Chad, and over the boundaries of Eritrea. Weak political systems and serious economic difficulties toppled governments. Civil war and outside intervention were often the result. Thus it was in Uganda and the Sudan.

The possession of resources—minerals and energy or vegetable resources—did not ensure stability. Development costs and profit invited competition for control. Governments in such states had no easy job asserting sovereignty, and hence the authority to negotiate with powerful business interests or states over the rights of resource exploitation. War was never far from the governments of new states and this did not change in the 1980s. Indeed war was the principal means by which government asserted its existence and administrative identity. Deny the government any administrative control and it, and the state, vanished. Many of the conflicts of the 1980s were about the existence of the state, and the ability of governments to carry out public administration. In the tenser and more violent places in the 1980s the reality of government and the state was threatened. This was the case in the Lebanon, even before the government of Israel felt obliged to intervene in 1982. The assassination of the President, Basir Gemayel, in 1982 was a symbol of the failure of administration and the collapse of the state. In Angola many parts of the territory were not controlled by the government but by rival forces during the 1980s. In Kampuchea, the Vietnamese swept aside an apparently ineffectual administration and in 1986 were still in virtual control of the larger part of the country. The war between Iran and Iraq began in 1980 as a result of an Iraqi assumption that Iranian rule was ineffective, and therefore that Iranian sovereignty could not be exercised in lands over which the Iraquis had a claim. This long-standing claim was thereupon asserted. The states of 1945 were able to impose their rule for the most part. By 1980 this was not the case and in this tumultuous world of states the policy of the two superpowers was uncertain.

The change came about in the 1980s. The role of the USA and the USSR in international politics had been reduced to narrow spheres of interest. These were not expanding, but had contracted. Until the end of the 1970s, the opposite had seemed to be true. The United States retained important influence. In the Middle East, Egypt, Israel and Saudi Arabia, even Iran until 1978, responded to that influential voice from Washington. But around 1980, this stopped. Egypt lost its political authority in the Arab world. In 1985 there were also clashes of view and interest between the United States and the Egyptian government over Palestinian terrorist activity. An Egyptian aircraft was diverted under threat by the Americans in October 1985 when carrying Palestinians associated with the hijacking of the Italian ship, *Achille Lauro*. That event had cost the life of an American citizen and thus prompted the interception of the Egyptian aircraft. Iran had ceased to be subject to any degree of American pressure, and the government of Israel had shown that there were limits to their subservience to the views of the USA. The invasion of the southern Lebanon was sustained against the expressed wishes of the American government and Congress in 1982. Close and easy relations with Saudi Arabia were not evident in the protracted debate in the USA on the supply of early warning radar systems (AWACS) during 1981.

The Soviet Union experienced a similar shrinking of influence and change in its international role in the 1980s. The apparent expansion of communist regimes after 1975 did not lead to a natural growth in Soviet influence. The USSR had a minimal role in the politics of the Middle East and their officials and citizens were equally subject to knidnap, as was seen in 1985. The Soviet Union had little ability to control policy in Angola or Mozambique. The government of the latter even reached an agreement with the government of South

Africa in 1984, relating to the control of insurgents in both countries. Both the governments of Angola and Mozambique negotiated trade and commercial deals with European and American companies, notably for the development and marketing of their natural resources. By 1985, the USSR had little impact in South-East Asia where racial and nationalist factors dominated politics, always at the expense of direct Soviet influence.

The first half of the decade, until 1985 and 1986, was therefore characterised by the reduction of superpower political clout. This amounted to the loss of joint dominion which had seemed so irreversible in international relations. In earlier years, direct mediation and pressure had limited conflict, or had helped to end war. The USSR and the United States had managed to achieve such results. Soviet mediation had ended war between India and Pakistan, and had contributed to the conference on Indo-China, albeit only temporarily successful, in Geneva in 1954. In 1979 President Carter brought about a reconciliation between the states of Israel and Egypt. He thereby achieved the apparently impossible. Mr Begin and President Sadat started discussions which led to the opening of frontiers, Israeli withdrawals from occupied territory and held out the prospect of full diplomatic recognition. Superpower restraining influence assisted in ending the fighting between Israel and Arab states in 1956, 1967 and 1973. But in the 1980s wars and international political disputes were not so readily controlled. Direct influence eluded the two superpowers for very particular reasons. This was most evident in the Middle and Near East. Negotiations failed in the years 1980–85 to end war and to assure the political future of the Palestinians. The United Nations, the government of the United States and locally influential Arab leaders, attempted to end the major conflicts in the region. Although the war between Iran and Iraq and the political destiny of the Palestinians were separate issues, no great progress was made in either matter. Five years of failed diplomacy left the parties further embedded in their political positions which had cost them five more years of casualties and pain in all cases.

None of the mediators had enough leverage. The United Nations offered no positive gain and no certainty of success.

The only force that could be applied was the presence of a peace-keeping unit. Some were stationed in the Middle East, interposed between Israel and other states and their armed forces. But these provided no political solution. Their tasks were not easy and they were often victims of attack or temporary capture, particularly those stationed in the Lebanon. Mediation by the Secretary General was not successful, although Mr Perez de Cuellar, like his predecessors, attempted to bring about the implementation of United Nations resolutions which had very wide support in New York where they were passed, but little among the parties concerned. The condemnation of acts against international law, and the demand for the return of lands gained by war (part of resolution 242), had little relevance in the face of miltary realities on the Golan Heights, the frontier between Israel and Syria, or on the vulnerable oil tankers which still sailed to the head of the Persian Gulf despite the war between Iran and Iraq and frequent attacks upon them by missiles.

The government of the USA also failed in its attempts to mediate. There was an uncritical assumption among peoples and governments of the region that the United States was strongly supportive of the government of Israel. In fact, it was the preservation of the state of Israel that formed the basis of the American view. The events of the 1980s showed the limits of support for particular Israeli policies by the government of the United States. However this criticism of Israeli action diminished the influence of the government of the United States. Criticism was directed at aspects of the Israeli invasion of the southern region of the Lebanon in Operation Peace for Galilee in 1982, undertaken by the armed forces in order to destroy bases of Palestinian terrorists who had made raids into Israel. In 1982 Congress had stopped the supply of aircraft and other military supplies to Israel in order to show its disapproval of the invasion and of the suspected Israeli connivance (or at least inertia) on the occasion of the massacres of Palestinians in refugee areas of Beirut, at Shatilla and Sabra. The Congressional ban was ineffective. The government of the United States had lost more ground as a mediator. Domestic pressure in the USA for support for Israel was strong. The government and Congress could not leave Israel to face the growing strength of the Arab states alone and the security of the state of Israel required military support. Moreover these were not the weapons that were used in the invasion of Lebanon.

The most promising attempts at negotiation seemed those of King Hussein of Jordan, who began a many-sided discussion of the issue of the Palestinian political future which included the governments of the United States and of Syria by 1985. He had a great interest in finding a political solution. There were more than 1 million Palestinians living in Jordan. He had had to crush the expanding and almost autonomous camps in 1970 with the Jordanian army, and by the 1980s the new expansion of camps threatened again to remove entire areas of the state of Jordan from the administrative control of the government. In 1985, negotiations were begun for the formal creation of a region within Jordan for Palestinians with their own administration. The vital question was policing and military control. King Hussein had an urgent need to find a secure and effective future for the Palestinians. But his initiative began to falter in the face of the military needs of the state of Israel: secure frontiers and internal security from terrorist raids, the determination of some Palestinian groups to base their political future in Israel, or on territory that was occupied by Israel, and in the face of the decreasing effective authority of the government of the Lebanon, notionally in the hands of Mr Gemayel since 1982. The fate of the state in the Lebanon was the most important factor diminishing superpower control in the area. The collapse of that state prevented a political solution.

Superpower influence had been based on the control of the flow of arms and their insistence on diplomatic settlement. This had never been easy, but it had been achieved, most notably in 1973. But this was no longer possible after 1979. The government of Egypt had been condemned by other Arab governments for negotiating with Israel. The Camp David agreement led to the ostracism of Egypt. The largest and most politically developed state in the region was thus diplomatically isolated. Only in 1984 were differences between the government of Egypt and the other Arab governments discussed at the Pan-Arab conference, held at Sunnae in North

Yemen in December. The Egyptians found themselves isolated. This isolation continued the following year, and the government of President Mubarak, who had come to power after the assassination of president Sadat by Islamic extremists in 1981, remained unable to bring direct and effective pressure. By this date, Egypt was also the main supporter of the United States in efforts to achieve a political settlement. The diplomatic focus had changed in another respect also. In 1948, 1956, 1967 and 1973, governments had been principally involved. Negotiations had been conducted with established states. In the 1980s this was no longer the case. Peace and a stable settlement were not dependent upon relatively stable governments like those of Egypt, Syria, Jordan and Israel. In the years 1980–85 the essential elements were not states. Regional instability was the result of the collapse of the state in the Lebanon and the presence of large numbers of Palestinians with no state or government of their own.

The Palestinian refugees in the Lebanon withered away the administrative control of the legitimate government. This occurred during the previous decade, once many thousands of Palestinians crossed into Lebanon from Jordan after their expulsion by King Hussein and his army. Many already lived in the Lebanon, but the arrival of more changed the political composition of the state. They took over parts of the state, built their own administration and policed their camps and village communities. This constituted a challenge to the government and the state. The traditionally Christian government of the Lebanon was therefore faced with a quite new population in these years. Older and established non-Christian communities in the towns and villages were also faced with the arrival of large numbers of Palestinians, often more militant than the majority. Many Palestinians also went to the vast capital city of Beirut, with a majority of Palestinians among the officially given population of 702,000. From the relative prosperity of the period before 1970, Lebanon became a land of war and economic decline. Employment collapsed; the unemployment rate was estimated to be 30 per cent. Participation in the various armed militias grew. In 1985 some estimates suggested that more than 5 per cent of the male population were engaged in these political and religious militias.[6] Governments had fallen, and leading politicians were driven into exile or assassinated. Many of the more commercially successful Lebanese, mostly from the Christian communities, emigrated. By 1985 the predominantly Christian areas had shrunk, and a Christian majority was only found in the proximity of Beirut. In short, the bases of the state of Lebanon had been destroyed or totally transformed in the decade 1975–85. No government sustained a sound grip on the administration of the state. The constant and personally courageous efforts of President Gemayal, after the assassination of his brother, were not successful. The need to remove all armed forces which owed his government no loyalty and over which his government exercised no sovereignty, preoccupied all parties. From 1982 to 1985 no certain source of political control existed. This confusion had provoked the Israeli invasion of 1982. Many of the Palestinian liberation fighters were expelled, under supervision, in 1984 and 1985, but others remained. Negotiations, begun in 1983, secured a slow withdrawal of most of the Israeli forces. Yet militia fighting continued, especially in Beirut, and the prospect of a Syrian enforcement of order remained likely. The Lebanese government had not achieved this by 1985, and the government of Israel remained determined to eliminate terrorist threats coming from an unruly Lebanon.

This 'fifth Middle Eastern war', as it has been called, demonstrated the failure of mediation. The government of the United States had attempted to lead the major parties towards an agreement between 1983 and 1985. The busy negotiations were led by the special presidential adviser, Mr Philip Habib, and in 1983–85 by the Secretary of State Mr George Schultz. They were both unsuccessful. In 1983 a conference held in Geneva brought together Israel, Saudi Arabia and Syria as well as Algeria, whose government had been successful in arranging the release of American hostages from Iran in 1981. But in the absence of a government in the Lebanon which could enforce order on the entire state, no secure settlement could be reached. The dispersal of many Palestinian fighters weakened the leadership of Yassir Arafat. There was no guarantee that he, or any other group or leader, could ensure obedience. The Palestinians were dispersed among many states by 1985, from

Tunisia and Libya to the states of the Persian Gulf. The Palestinian Liberation Organisation moved its headquarters to Tunis, where the centre was attacked by Israeli aircraft in 1985 and largely destroyed. Other important Palestinian groups continued to operate from almost all Arab states, and some of the smaller units were still able to continue fighting and kidnapping many Americans, French, British and Russians, after the dispersal of many of the activists. Other groups in addition to the Palestinians also engaged in this activity against foreigners.

The impotence of external governments in the search for peace in the Lebanon was tragically shown by the experience of the four-power military force, invited to Beirut by the government of the Lebanon in 1983. Although the Soviet Union was not involved, American troops were joined by those of France, Italy and the United Kingdom. The experiment was therefore one of great power intervention if not of superpower control. They were finally shown to be irrelevant rather than a failure. Bomb attacks on the bases of the American marines and the French forces, causing hundreds of deaths, brought the peace effort to an end. The last of the forces were withdrawn in February 1984. In the absence of a secure state, great powers could do nothing, and as the tensions persisted an acceptable political solution became more difficult to find.

During the 1980s an additional and important factor limited great power and superpower action, and discouraged their intervention. Costs rose with intimidating speed as conflicts lengthened. Congress was especially wary of the results of authorising any intervention by the troops of the United States. The increasing costs were usually a result of the quantity and complexity of equipment, but by no means always. In the seemingly endless fighting in Chad, the major costs were logistic and for the replacement of basic vehicles not sophisticated aircraft. A French journalist called the war in northern Chad, that of the Toyota and the Land-Rover. Trucks and fourwheeled-drive vehicles were essential items. Much the same was true in the Polisario war in the Western Sahara. The periodic major intervention of French forces in Chad merely cost the French government larger amounts of money. By 1985 a further 1000 troops were required for operation 'Epermer'; the attack on the airstrip at Ouadi-Doum suggested yet greater future costs. Therefore the tremendous costs and lengthy conflicts demanded caution from the superpowers and limited their intervention. But this also limited their influence.

There were few good arguments for a superpower intervention in the war between Iran and Iraq. The change of regime in Iran deprived the United States of influence in Teheran, as it did the British who had been friends of the Shah and the military suppliers of Iranian forces. The nature and expensive attrition rate of equipment in the war discouraged involvement on either side. The Soviet Union had no strong argument for intervention. Costs were again too high, and there was no historical basis on which to build a close association. Moreover the Ayatollah's regime had spurned both Western and Communist states. In addition only influence of a minor kind linked the USSR to the Iraqi government in Baghdad where Soviet arms had been bought. The Soviet ally in the region was Syria, and political, religious and territorial issues divided the Syrian and Iraqi governments. The Syrians were suspected of providing some military assistance to the government of Iran with which there were strong religious ties. The more populist kind of Islamic organisation favoured in Iran and which gave the religious leaders, the Mullahs, their great authority, was alien to Iraq. But this was shared by the Syrians, and therefore despite the Ayatollahs' denunciation of communism, there was scope for future political agreement, and the completion, in effect, of the reversal of alliances. By 1985 this had not happened.

France became the most important partner for Iraq and the crucial supplier of arms. At the start of the war in 1980, the aircraft and weapons of the Iraqi forces were predominantly Soviet, the remainder French. Resupply came from France and from other Arab states, thus there was a slight increase in dependence on France. The Iranians had acquired the largely British and American equipment of the Shah's regime. This was more expensive to maintain and difficult to replace. The costs of resupply were very great. The aircraft in particular were expensive to service and re-arm. The Iraqi aircraft, including modern French Mirage with Exocet missiles, were engaged in up to 500 sorties each day. The Iranians, with 255 F-4 fighters and over 500 helicopters, and a constant need for more Sparrow and Sidewinder missiles, had similarly costly demands. Such expenses effectively excluded any military support from outside. No single regime could afford it. The stalemate which developed, with forces bogged down in the marshes of the frontier area, at the head of the Persian Gulf, suggested only a long war.

The war had begun in 1980. It proved one of the more bloody and turgid of recent wars. Thousands of young men were left dying on the straggling front in the contested lands. For five years only marginal gains were made, with towns and barren regions exchanging hands. High hills to the north and marshes below, with no proper crossing points and bridges, ruled out tank warfare. Key objectives like the Iranian oil bases at the head of the Gulf, and the main road connecting Basra and Baghdad, remained the principal targets. In this war no real advantage was gained. The optimism of the Iraqi government and Revolutionary Council which encouraged the original offensive and reopened an old dispute, was unjustified. Between September 1981 and June 1982, the larger Iranian army of approximately 280,000 regained their grip. Although Iraq kept pressure on the oilfields and the terminals and shipping, the supplies began to flow again and continued, preventing a total economic collapse in Iran. The Haag Island terminal became vital and kept fighting located to the head of the Gulf. No clear victory seemed likely, yet the Iranians insisted on the destruction of the Iraqi regime, rejecting a negotiated settlement. External intervention was difficult. The two states were large and not easily amenable to influence. Iran, with more than 36 million inhabitants, had the largest population of any state between North Africa and the Asian sub-continent—a population size shared with Egypt. Iraq, with 12 million, was the third largest state in the region. The political structures and the serious regional problems of both, made an external intervention risky because unpredictable. The secessionist war with the Kurds in the north of Iran and Iraq continued, and Iran had other regional pressures. The war was thus allowed to continue.

The fear of creating a political imbalance also kept the

superpowers away. Any strong support for either the USA or the USSR would have threatened the fragile stability of the entire area and neither had jeopardised their position. The example of the change in political allegiance by the government of Egypt between 1973 and 1978, and the Camp David agreement, had shown the dangers of involvement in the affairs of an established state by one of the superpowers. In addition, the lesson of the Soviet experience in Egypt and the American experience in Iran, in which so much political and military capital had been invested, were salutary. In both cases, years of work were destroyed almost overnight. The blow to the nature of superpower influence was great; theirs was a precarious role and impotence during the war between Iran and Iraq stressed the point. The costs of involvement were great. The United States had discovered this in Vietnam, and the Soviet Union in Afghanistan. Any operation in the Middle or Near East was on a scale quite different from the occupation of the island of Grenada, small, brief and completely controllable. For this reason, the intricacy of local political pressures and the military realities contributed to the diminishing international role of the superpowers. Therefore in the Middle East the gap between the power of the United States and of the USSR and the reality of their political impact was sharply revealed in the 1980s.

An important difference existed between the United States' intervention in the island of Grenada and its part in the four power mission in Beirut in 1983–84. In the Caribbean example, as elsewhere in Central America, a determining influence could be brought. Washington offered cooperation or acknowledged and tolerated ideological differences, as in the case of the Cuban Republic. Stability and economic development depended on the attitude of the United States. When it was thought that instability threatened, as in the Grenadan example, Washington could invade and enforce its own solution. No other government was directly involved. The operation was carried out with sufficient force to ensure success, and the chance was provided for a new legitimate government to establish its authority. The majority of American troops had gone home after a rapid and successful operation on 15 December, although a few medical, training, police and support troops remained.

A legitimate government had also invited the four-power intervention in Beirut, but success was dependent upon the effective exercise of sovereignty by the government. That was not possible and 279 American soldiers died as a result, as did almost as many French troops. Practical constraints on their actions, a non-combattant role and largely patrolling mission, meant that the troops were not defending the state nor enhancing its immediate authority. The use of the four-power force was to protect the parameters of the state administered by the Gemayel government, to allow it to rebuild and improve its authority and policing. They had no real scope for autonomous action as in Grenada. Moreover attacks on the American and French units were more likely than on the British and Italian troops, since the latter were not regarded as politically partial and committed, as were the former. Both USA and France had a history of involvement in the Lebanon; the United States had landed troops there as recently as 1958. Both governments were known to have defined political obligations in the Middle East—the USA in relation to Israel, France in relation to Iraq. However all the units were placed in a similar position, invited to protect an authority which manifestly did not exist and which they were not constitutionally empowered nor militarily equipped to impose. Their role was thus significantly weak and they were withdrawn in February 1984.

The great powers barely existed as such if they were unable to support a government that invited their intervention. They were effective as superpowers only if their military strength enhanced the authority of a government. The United States learned this in Vietnam. In the 1980s, this was only achieved in their established spheres of interest. The USA could not intervene in Africa as easily as in Central America because no political basis existed. After the success of the Sandinistas in Nicaragua in 1979, the government in Washington was concerned to show the secure constitutional authority of the governments in El Salvador and the Honduras. The proper conduct of elections in 1983 in the former, and 1985 in the latter, was stressed by the United States to lend integrity to their aid programme. The Soviet Union was in a similar position. Its international role was safest in the preserve of Eastern Europe, and perhaps also when exercised at the request of a sympathetic government like that of Afghanistan, even if carefully stage-managed.

However during the 1980s neither the Soviet Union nor the United States could ensure control in regions normally regarded as their spheres of influence. The Soviet Union was unable to end war in East Africa and South-East Asia where belligerent states were dependent on Soviet support for at least short-term military supply. Not only was a clear political interest not always apparent, it was not always possible to bring influence to bear. In East Africa, the Soviet Union switched alignment from Somalia to Ethiopia, just as the government of President Carter would abandon the regime of Anastasio Somoza in Nicaragua a year later, in 1978. Secure allies were not easily found in the Third World. In 1985 and 1986 the government of the Honduras denied the claim of Washington that Nicaraguan troops had crossed their borders. Trouble, risk and the fear of making irrevocable commitments in policies were present in all of these conflicts, and they undermined the policies of the superpowers. Furthermore, many of the wars and endemic violence of the 1980s were lengthy and eluded negotiated settlement. The Soviet Union was involved in talks in Geneva intended to end the war in Afghanistan; by 1986 no basis for peace had been found. France was repeatedly sucked into the civil war in Chad, a process that had begun in 1965 and showed no signs of ending. Similarly, wars in the Western Sahara, Kampuchea, in southern Africa and Central America had been constant through the decade 1975–85. The extended nature of these conflicts worked against likely intervention by the superpowers. Their ability to bring an end to fighting was seriously diminished, although some might have doubted that the ability ever really existed.

Both the United States and the Soviet Union faced other changes in international relations. The seemingly permanent alliances that had been created as a part of the policy of containment and as a response to that policy, disappeared or changed radically. Only NATO and the Warsaw Pact remained in their Cold War form. The institutions which had locked the world into a divided system for defence and security, had completely altered by 1980.

The close link between the Chinese People's Republic and the Soviet Union, bound by a common ideology and understanding of international politics, had been broken. Their troops had clashed on the contested frontier in central Asia, and by the late 1970s the Soviet Union had deployed SS 20 missiles on their border. Although new negotiations had been begun in the 1980s, relations were still hostile and suspicious, with the People's Republic edging closer in commercial and political relations to partners in the Pacific basin, and Japan and the USA in particular. The stability of the 1950s had vanished. In many respects the Soviet Union found itself more isolated in the decade after the end of the Vietnam War and the unification of that state by the communist government of the North. Commercial ties existed between the USSR and several communist states, notably Cuba, Vietnam, Nicaragua and Ethiopia; these scarcely served as a secure system of alliances. The links were fragile and the states widely spread about the globe. There was an air of *ad hoc* arrangements about these relations, lacking the stability of an alliance system. Only the long-standing bilateral treaty arrangement with Syria gave the Soviet Union a solid ally. The agreement between the Soviet Union and the government of Iraq for the supply of arms before 1980 had turned into an embarrassing and clumsy burden once the war started with Iran. Soviet policy was neither sure nor consistent with the earlier policy. In this region also the assumptions of previous decades did not apply after 1980.

The alliances that grew from containment and were directed by the government of the United States also changed dramatically. The Central Treaty Organisation did not survive the fall of the Shah's regime in Iran. The pressures which had affected the organisation ensured that without Iran, little meaning existed for this arrangement. Too many American resources had been used by CENTO governments for domestic repression or local interests rather than as the basis of deterrence in the Near East. Military aid to Turkey had been stopped by Congress after the invasion of Cyprus by the Turks in 1974, only gradually resumed five years later. After 1979, evidence became clear that military equipment had been used for internal repression in Iran during the Shah's regime. The

South-East Asian Treaty Organisation crumbled with the failure of American policy in Vietnam. The ANZAS agreement was strained by the refusal of the New Zealand government of Mr Lange to allow access to New Zealand waters to nuclear-powered ships. The fleets of the United States were directly affected. The strong opposition to nuclear weapons and nuclear-propelled ships limited the role of the United States in the region. The attitude of the New Zealand government and the support which Mr Lange received was strengthened by the determination of the French government to continue testing nuclear weapons in the Pacific. In 1985 the ship 'Rainbow Warrior', of the environmental group Greenpeace, vigorously opposed to the testing and deployment of nuclear arms, was sabotaged in the harbour at Auckland, New Zealand. The principal suspects were agents of the French secret service, and the affair resulted in the resignation of the Minister of Defence, Charles Hernu. The death of a photographer who had been on board the 'Rainbow Warrior' and the intervention with such damaging and tragic results by the French official agencies, served only to harden feelings in the South Pacific against nuclear weapons, and directed criticism at governments whose military strategies depended upon nuclear arms. For the USA strategy was less stable as hostility to their nuclear-powered ships developed.

Wars slipped from superpower control as the details of national foreign and defence policies were determined less by global ideology than the need to maintain public order. Even military supply did not guarantee unconditional political influence, as the Soviet Union found in relations with Iraq after 1980. In 1982 the war between the United Kingdom and the Argentine exposed superpower weakness.

No substantial issue was then at stake between the Soviet Union and the United States in the South Atlantic in 1982. The economic ties between the USSR and the Argentine had not damaged the economic interests of the United States. Indeed the government in Washington suffered the burden of close relations with both belligerents. The United Kingdom was the major European ally of the United States, with especially friendly relations between the leaders on both sides of the Atlantic, President Reagan and Mrs Thatcher. The involvement of the United States in the Argentine had become more extensive until the economic relationship was of the greatest importance to the latter, a trade that included major armaments supply. Although trade with the Soviet Union had increased rapidly by 1980, this was confined to Argentinian exports. The major trading partner, if imports were taken into account, remained the USA in 1982, and this position had a political importance. The government of the United States could not allow the Soviet Union to encroach on traditional American markets nor threaten the motherly role that governments in Washington liked to play in relation to the states of Latin America. The extension of Soviet commercial interests in 1980 therefore came at a moment when conflict was especially undesirable for the USA. Good relations with Latin American governments required constant and assiduous effort. The war in the South Atlantic therefore tore United States' loyalties in different directions.

The immediate cause of the war was the Argentinian occupation of the British base in South Georgia as a first step in asserting an old claim to sovereignty over the island. Then came the invasion of the more important settlement at Port Stanley. The assertion of a claim in international law by invasion was a principle that could be condemned by the government in Washington. But the USA had at least an ambiguous view about the sovereignty of the Falklands/ Malvinas Islands and had no desire to ruffle relations with Argentina at a time when the Soviet Union was becoming a more significant factor in Latin American politics. Moreover the military regime in the Argentine was already under pressure from public criticism and Congressional scrutiny on its performance on human rights. Too many opponents had vanished without trace in the few years before the war, and the distressing record of the military regime was revealed publicly in 1983 and 1984 when the democratic government led by Mr Alfonsin replaced it after the surrender in the Falklands. The fighting between the Argentinians and the British was thus a delicate matter for the government in the United States. There was little possibility for immediate and totally unambiguous support for the United Kingdom. The war threatened to destroy years of political effort.

Latin American states, with the exception of the government of Chile, were solid in their support for the Argentine. The issue of sovereignty was an opportunity for the USA to show its solidarity with the major part of the rest of the hemisphere. Few states from outside had taken such an active forceful step as did the British in defence of their interests in the Falklands since Louis Napoleon in 1862. Failure to defend the integrity of the region and to proclaim the inviolability of the Monroe Doctrine, that no external intervention would be tolerated by the government of the United States in the Americas, put the Latin American interests of the USA at risk. Although there were many different types of government in Latin America—military regimes, quasi-parliamentary governments and Marxist regimes—they shared a sense of mistrust of the United States and dependence on the economic and military weight of the northern part of the hemisphere. No simple ideological pattern applied. A military junta could lean towards the Soviet Union; a democratic government could criticise the United States. The Latin American states needed to assert their independence as well as draw as much aid as possible from the USA. The unity in support of the Argentinians in 1982 was directed at the government in Washington as much as at the United Kingdom. The sensitive nature of the political complexion of Latin America was shown in 1985, when a Social-Democratic and self-styled 'revolutionary' government in Peru, was under attack from Maoist insurgents (the Path of Light movement) and was also critical of the policies of the United States. There was every need for the United States to encourage movement away from the radicalism of insurgent groups and the dead hand of military dictatorships such as that which had begun the war in the Falklands in 1982. The political role for the government of President Reagan was therefore essentially a cautious one. He needed a peaceful settlement of the dispute. But there was little basis on which the United States and the Secretary of State, General Haig, could build a compromise. Political expediency, loyalty to an important European ally and disapproval of first resort to force, were hard to balance and use as the foundation for mediation. Thus the attempted mediation by the United States was unsuccessful, as was that attempted by the Secretary

General of the United Nations, Mr Perez de Cuellar. Without a defined path towards a mediated settlement, the only solution was that of war. In the case of the Falklands, such an outcome was relatively rapidly achieved. The USA offered minor military assistance to the United Kingdom—some equipment and resupply, cooperation on the Ascension Island airbase, and an unspecified amount of signals and intelligence help. All this was provided at the risk of future US interests in Latin America, although the change of government in the Argentine, the return to democracy under the premiership of Mr Alfonsin, and the condemnation of the military oligarchy that had initiated the war, spared the United States some of the opprobrium of having supported the British. However, the significance was clear that the USA could only endorse the need for a military solution. The United States was unable to play a political role; the only effective policy was to await the outcome of the war and in this way the erosion of international control by a superpower was further encouraged.

As in the conflicts in the Near and Middle East, of which there were several during the years after the Camp David agreement and the collapse of the Pahlovi dynasty in Iran, the only effective arbiter was war. Yet war in the 1980s had slipped further from superpower control as had their ability to mediate in international disputes. The former role of the superpowers was dependent on an awareness of the indivisibility of events in international relations. War in one state or region inevitably affected peace elsewhere. Seemingly insignificant events turned out to be part of the ideological and balance of power struggle between the East and West. The indivisible world that had been hinted at by Mr Chamberlain in 1938, referring to the faraway state of Czechoslovakia, and accepted as self-evident as war and its results impinged on all lives, began to change around 1980. Although the presence of the Soviet Union and the United States, and the hands of their agencies, the KGB and the CIA, had been suspected everywhere, this had begun to vanish. The interconnection between events was broken and no longer so clear-cut. Whereas the victory of the insurgents led by Fidel Castro in Cuba in 1959 had consequences far beyond the change of government on a Caribbean island, such global impact was less obvious in 1980. The global importance of events only became evident if the two superpowers could impose their logic on those events. In many of the wars and conflicts this was not possible in the way that it had occurred in Vietnam, in Korea, in the Congo or even in Angola and the events of the 1970s in Ethiopia, Somalia and the Sudan. The superpowers were seriously hampered.

NOTES

1. The *Force d'action et d'assistance rapide* consisted of some 7600 troops in 45 units, stationed in France and in states which were formerly part of the French Empire in Africa. *Le Monde* 11 July 1985.
2. Carlo Rossella, 'Armi e buoi dei paesi tuoi', *Panorama,* 13 April 1986. The author quotes extensively from the work of Thoma Ohlson of the Stockholm Institute for Peace Research, and from other recent surveys.
3. This was the figure approved by Congress in October 1985. The defence budget of the United States is not presented as a single item or figure, but consists of several headings.
4. From $1.2 billion to *c.*$4.0 billion in 1984/85. This and comparable figures are provided annually in the surveys published by the International Institute for Strategic Studies in London.
5. Ibid.
6. 'Chrétiens du Liban', *Le Monde,* 27–28 October 1985.

6 Politics and Ideology

A world dominated by two superpowers implied and even required the indivisibility of international politics. Nothing happened in isolation. War and peace in any region had global consequences. Moreover the bipolarity which the exceptional powers of the United States and the Soviet Union had created, also suggested the continuing relevance of a commitment to capitalism and communism. Neither the Soviet government nor that of the Reagan administration abandoned the idea of indivisibility. Their attitudes and rhetoric reinforced it.

Some degree of belief in the indivisibility of international politics always existed in the Soviet view of politics. War was essentially a capitalist phenomenon as Lenin had argued. The fundamental conflict between capitalism and the progressive forces emerged through war. Particular circumstances might distort the underlying struggle against communism, but this would finally be revealed. Soviet versions of the causes of war in Afghanistan developed this theme. A loyal regime in Kaboul was alleged to have been subverted by imperialist scheming, and the gains made since the Marxist *coup d'état* of 1978 were threatened.

Generations of Americans also believed in an interrelated and indivisible world. In its early formulation, the idea of an interdependent world after 1945 meant fighting communism everywhere for the preservation of 'western' values. This view of international relations was quite as all-bracing as that of the Soviets. Moreover the shift towards a policy of détente did not destroy the former presuppositions. Above all members of the many administrations of the United States, Dr Henry Kissinger retained an apparent belief in the unity of international politics. Peace in Vietnam would be related to the bringing of peace elsewhere. After 1978, and especially after the change of regime in 1981, the view still prevailed that the USSR remained committed to a global policy, exploiting weaknesses and seeking advantages for the pursuit and encouragement of social systems sympathetic towards the Soviet Union. Their officials in Ethiopia and in Angola, in the South Yemen and in Libya seemed to bear witness to this assessment of Soviet aims. But a break in this linkage had occurred, although this might not be immediately apparent. President Reagan was reported to have enjoyed the swashbuckling and taciturn opponent of world communism depicted in the series of *Rambo* films. This simple pleasure also revealed an implicit and sustained belief in the unity and coherence of international relations. Yet political changes in those relations undermined the conviction that the world retained that unity and consistency which had first been accepted in 1945.

A radical change in international politics was brought about by the developments of the 1970s. Competition between the Soviet Union and the United States was less keen after the specific agreements of the period of détente. Global rivalry was initially no longer so necessary or so nervous. With the decrease in tension between the superpowers came a new relationship both between the USA and the USSR and between each of these states and the rest of the world. The conditions which had existed since the end of the Second World War vanished. The global relationships were not sharpened by the divisions of the Cold War, but smoothed and honed by détente and the alluring prospects of new relationships which were offered. By no means all states chose to opt for one side or the other of the old divide. Governments traded with both, and drew inspiration and benefit from their relations with both. American and West European companies penetrated further into Marxist economies. Communists fought communists in other states. Soviet weapons were bought by military oligarchies. The patterns were infinite.

In May 1982, the French newspaper *Le Monde* published an article by the author, and now editor of the paper, André Fontaine. The argument developed the theme of what M.

Fontaine called 'la fin du condominium', the domination of international politics by the United States and the Soviet Union. The failure of the dialogue between North and South, the collapse of price stability and the spread and virulence of local wars, were the substance. The very nature and notion of superpowers were called into question by the disappearance of a clear division in international relations. Their shared influence had declined and the results of this virtual disappearance were experienced during the 1980s.

The decade began with widely expressed fears in the United States that the Soviet Union had gained significant political advantage. The balance between the superpowers had tilted in favour of the USSR since 1973. The implication was that the degree of imbalance was so great that international tensions had been increased.

The argument was bluntly stated by President Reagan in an answer to a press question in 1981: 'so far détente's been a one-way street that the Soviet Union has used to pursue its own aims . . . they reserve unto themselves the right to commit any crime, to lie, to cheat, in order to attain their goal of a socialist state'.[1] Within the almost Biblical language was the suggestion that separate national goals and interests were pursued at the expense of international stability and compromise. Even critics of the policies of the United States during the late 1970s and the first years of the Republican administration, agreed that the USSR had managed to claw some advantage from the years of détente, particularly in the military and trade balance.[2] In principle this was not surprising: 'Détente heightens competition between communist and democratic way of life in East and West'.[3]

Many Americans had a sense of humiliation and disadvantage in relation to the Soviet Union in 1980. This undoubtedly helped to bring a Republican victory in the presidential elections. The Iranian dramas òf 1977–79 showed the failure of the USA to sustain a competitive policy. Intelligence reports failed to convey the nature of the domestic crisis in Iran. Washington underestimated the significance of Islamic fervour, of popular hostility towards the Shah's regime and the police. The collapse of the dynasty appeared to come as a surprise and left the military alliance in disorder. The later failure to rescue hostages at the embassy in Teheran, and further casualties during the attempt, emphasised the lost initiative of the government. The suspicion that Soviet benefit came from American impotence was generally encouraged by such events.

The sense of political frustration and national humiliation coincided with the knowledge that the Soviet Union had not stopped the expansion and development of its military capacity. During these years the Soviet missile systems were modernised, and the European governments were made aware of the nature of the new weapons and their direct threat to the cities and installations of the western alliance. The assumption that détente might imply a reduction in arms was shown to have been an illusion. Arms control and arms discussions invited the development of new and alternative means of defence. They could result in a clear expansion of military power. The Soviet Union had manifestly appreciated this logic. Thus international relations between the superpowers had lost a sense of balance between 1973 and 1980. Moreover several states had acquired communist governments. They were found in those regions where the United States government could not easily intervene. In South-East Asia the nightmare that afflicted French regular officers—Marshall de Lattre de Tassigny's fear of states falling like dominoes to communism—was almost realised. By 1975 all of Vietnam was communist. The clashes between the Khmer Rouge and the Vietnamese continued to 1985, with the steady assertion of Vietnamese rule in Kampuchea. Communist insurgents were active in Laos and Thailand. They had spread to Burma and were active in the Philippines. A similar pattern seemed to be occurring in Africa. In central and southern Africa, the drift towards communism was certain, in Angola, Mozambique, Ethiopia. The Soviet Union had gained important allies and political advantage in other states—South Yemen, Nicaragua, perhaps even Grenada, and certainly in Afghanistan. The net gain in political influence had gone to the USSR. In addition, the Soviet Union had improved its relative military position, with the expansion of its navy, increases in airborne divisions, and the development, production and deployment of new missiles. Soviet political influence brought an end to the war between India and Pakistan over the secession of the territory of Bangladesh in 1975, and they used their naval facilities to clear the blocked harbour at Chittagong. Economic benefits had come to the USSR from the expansion of trade and investment with West Europe in the 1970s. Their 'surrogates', as President Reagan called them, were operating in Chad, Angola, East Germans in Ethiopia and South Yemen.

However what became clearer in the 1980s was that the gain and loss analysis in international politics was of diminishing importance. It had become less relevant to relations between the United States and the Soviet Union than other factors. This was partly because there had been a relative decline in the international dominance of the two ideologies. Neither communism nor liberal democracy and its free-market principles collapsed in the face of newly assertive ideologies. The Soviet system and the political economies of many of the states associated with the USSR, managed to adapt to the investment from the West and the lively commerce that existed between the states of the East and the West. Western Europe, the United States and the powerful economy of Japan in the Far East, all demonstrated a remarkable resilience. The slide towards the political left and the appearance of 'euro-communism' which seemed so strong in the middle of the 1970s had been reversed. Communist parties were in decline. The feared economic collapse did not happen. Capitalism swept forward with the Japanese leading world production of motor cars, and many of the microelectronics required by the innovations of the 1980s. The experience of France, where a socialist president was elected in 1981, and a socialist government survived until the legislative elections of 1986, turned into a further triumph of French technology. France remained firmly within the liberal market economies of the European Community, sharing improved industrial growth, a steady export performance and technical innovation.

The principles to which the superpowers appealed were still relevant to the organisation of their different social systems. The principles also remained quite distinct, but this difference so acutely understood in Washington and Moscow, was less clear to others. The single-party socialist economies had considerable experience of the trade and investment with free-market states, and there was nothing inconsistent in this development. A degree of market operation was also perfectly applicable within the overall economic structure of so-called communist states. There was an extension of this factor in Hungary, and private ownership in all such states.[4] On the other hand, intervention and careful control of the market were not inconsistent with capital accumulation and the nurturing of the profit motive. Indeed the market required regulation, order and social responsibility in order to function 'freely'. Periodic intervention on the exchange markets was not destructive of free-market policies, and this was practised by the Reagan administration. Growth and the flowering of choice and markets were actually assisted by a degree of intervention which ensured that a dollar bought tomorrow what it could buy today; this was described by Dr Sprinkel, chairman of the President's Council of Economic Advisers in 1985/86, as the maintenance of 'an honest dollar'.

Social-Democratic politicians in many states blended interventionist policies and the truly free market. The precise mix varied, but many governments were influenced by the European model, and in particular by the idea of a social market economy. The Social-Democratic government in Peru, the APRA administration elected in 1985, was just such an example, applying policies which varied from state control of industries to the encouragement of market forces and freer trade. Much the same applied in Brazil which had a new democratic government replacing the military regime. Market forces and traditional economic liberalism were not in principle opposed to specific regulatory policies like an incomes policy. The logic behind many, if not even a majority, of multi-party democracies was that occasional intervention was necessary in order to protect the uncluttered and incorrupt market. This logic demanded the protection of the more exposed elements. This was the policy of individual governments and of the European Community which protected poorer regions, declining sectors and inefficient farmers in this way. The idea of the social market economy was not socialist or left-of-centre; it originated with the West German Christian Democrats, notably the former Chancellor Dr Ludwig Erhard. The market had responsibilities towards its customers. Their welfare and their incomes needed safeguards for the market to continue to function effectively. The precise method of such regulation was the subject of political debate, and it was not easy to sustain a high degree of social control and income protection and allow free development of new business and experiment. What was clear in the 1980s was the continuing appeal of the middle ground. In these circumstances, a division between capitalism and communism was an anachronism, a stark contrast with an altogether different relevance. Many political leaders viewed the organisation of the economy and the state from outside these categories.

The once obvious differences between East and West were less sharp in the 1980s. The relations between states moved according to other principles although the operations of one power were still felt by all the rest. The peoples of the world needed constant reminders of the differences between social systems and what these differences meant for social policy, security from war and violence and for their environment. They were by no means easily convinced. Neither the Soviet regime nor the experts in the West carried total conviction when they explained and commented upon such events as the Soviet nuclear power station accident at Chernobyl, in April 1986. The context in which governments operated was felt to be alien and different from the international relations of 1945.

Strains developed in the relations between the two giant powers of the USA and the Soviet Union and their respective allies. The subject of harmony within alliances became a recurrent theme, although not a new one. Non-aligned and uncommitted governments regarded the two superpowers differently. Economic factors and the world-wide pressures for a new protectionism divided states on lines which had less connection with East/West distinctions than before. The apparent growth of uncontrollable violence and aggression was aggravated by the erosion of Soviet and American political influence. The influence of these states remained essentially material, or it had become so. They were ideological leaders only with difficulty and no longer with conviction. They were clearly leaders in technical, military and economic matters. Therefore the primary place of Cold War or détente had receded. An analysis of events which still stressed those former profound currents in international relations risked giving an emphasis to Soviet and United States interests and policies which these did not deserve. Soviet–American relations might be stressed at the expense of other forces. The conclusion of this work is that Cold War and détente have become terms without relevance or precise meaning in the 1980s. Cold War was eroded almost as soon as it appeared, holding the seeds of its decline. The jump from an event like the Cuban missiles crisis in October 1962, to the 'hot-line' between Moscow and Washington was bridged by the need to prevent war. Once recognised as a guiding principle for policy, détente too was challenged by the need to secure advantage, and deterioration began long before Mr Reagan ran for the presidency of the USA. However no definite and unequivocal return to Cold War occurred. There was always a demand for new talks and for greater harmony. But the relations between capitalism and communism did not dominate diplomatic discussion in the 1980s. The leaders of the industrial free-market states were not preoccupied with the policies of the closed economies. The agendas of their regular meetings showed concern with the need to sustain growth and employment, to prevent restrictive practices by their own governments or protective policies by those states with the primary resources necessary for economic expansion. Cold War preoccupations were secondary.

No single moment or event dismissd both Cold War and détente to the world of international history rather than leave them relevant to the study of contemporary international relations. Détente was probably less secure and shorter in duration than many hoped. The arrival of North Vietnamese troops in Saigon in 1975 was perhaps the nearest event to a turning-point, after which Cold War and détente were both dead, to be replaced by a new international political order in which the former superpowers behaved differently.

The heart of the changed world which came to fruition in the 1980s was the relative ease with which superpower influence could be avoided. In earlier years the burden of superpower influence was inescapable. Alignment with either the United States or the Soviet Union came to any new regime no matter how it had come into power, whether by constitutional or by revolutionary means. Thus the wavering of Fidel Castro's Cuban revolution in 1959–60 was finally resolved and the regime leaned towards Moscow. Mr Nehru's non-aligned or Third World ideal took many years to create with any measure of security. It had remained an ideal only until international changes encouraged the formation of truly non-aligned policies.

The changes were clear. Soviet impact on the communist movement became diluted. The gap between Soviet practice and Maoist principles opened in the years 1950–60. By 1980 there were several blends of Marxism in the world of single-party communist politics. In Europe there was growing stress on the different paths to socialism. While the military alliance of the Warsaw Pact stayed secure, Hungarians and Poles explored different styles of socialist economics and politics. The Soviet model had few lessons for coordinated union activity and political demands, or for the injection of market preferences and foreign commerce on the scale proposed and advanced by the Hungarian government. Outside Europe it was not clear how far the Soviet model was relevant to Angola or Ethiopia, to Nicaragua or Afghanistan.

The world of the 1980s was also different for the non-communist states. Japan and the European Community which added a further 50 million inhabitants to a free-market community in the 1980s, represented new challenges to the trade of both superpowers. These economies were expanding in directions that the Soviet Union could not match. Their successful levels of growth and the strong elements of protectionism in policy by both these economic giants, affected planned and liberal economies. The USA no longer dominated the world economy as had been the case in the 1950s and 1960s. The context in which the government of the United States attempted to secure a strong dollar had changed. The value of the currency was determined by forces beyond the control of Washington, notably by the price of oil, calculated in dollars. Moreover, the rapid development of new production techniques and the huge increase in the market for new kinds of product, brought commercial success in the 1980s to many states that were also closely associated with the Japanese market. They either competed with the Japanese companies or entered manufacturing by filling the gaps left by the Japanese industry. This commercial success in the Far East transformed trading and the prosperity of the countries in which it occurred (South Korea, Taiwan and Singapore) as it did the place of the USA and the Soviet Union in the Pacific basin. In addition, the shift of political and economic energies to the East was encouraged by the opening of the market in the People's Republic of China after the death of Mao Tse Tung. Buyer and developing producer, this state further vitalised the economies of many Pacific states, not least the United States and Japan. The opportunities were quickly grasped. The irony was that the economic goals of the Japanese empire in the 1930s—trade domination of the China coast and access secured to primary materials from the weaker territories of the South China Seas—were attained in large measure in the 1980s. But this time there was no war.

The United States also began to shift economic priorities. The Americans became influential in the markets of the Far East and suppliers of arms to most states in the Pacific basin, including the People's Republic of China. The origins were clear before 1980, but accelerated after the Reagan administration came to power, with its roots, like those of the new President, embedded on the West Coast. By the middle of the decade, the Soviet Union also was interested in the region. New approaches towards the Chinese regime were noted over a number of years, and continued after the arrival of the younger leadership of Mr Gorbachev. Fishing and other mutually beneficial agreements were signed with a few regimes and some political movements. Such were the contracts with the former Gilbert Islands for considerable fishing privileges, signed in 1985. The Soviet Union was also rumoured to have contacts with dissident groups in the Philippines and in New Caledonia, as were the Cubans in Fiji.[5] The result was not simply the arrival of the Cold War in the Pacific, but the establishment of new priorities for the government of the United States.

The search for stability and order in international politics moved away from the desire for détente between the United States and the Soviet Union. The prospect of talks between their leaders was secondary, and could not achieve the aim of world peace. Despite the many public statements that accompanied the preparations for the Geneva summit of November 1985, and the talks between Mr Gorbachev and President Reagan, and the yet more public anticipation of future talks at that level, world peace was not dependent upon these two men and the powerful governments that they represented. Geneva was no Yalta. The balance between the separate gains and losses of the two powers that once shared global dominance, could not guarantee the stable and orderly world as it had done in the years of Cold War and détente. There were two aspects to this development in international politics.

The first was that it was no longer easy to establish gains and losses. The ambiguity of the Soviet position in Africa, both in the southern region and in the Horn of Africa, was more significant than the former assumption of a straightforward Soviet advantage, taken during the period of détente. The same ambiguity existed in other regions where there were few stable governments and secure states, in Central America and the Caribbean islands, in the Middle East and in North Africa. Therefore, new policies were required from both Washington and Moscow.

The second aspect of the diminishing importance of superpower balance in the 1980s, was the emergence of dynamic new political forces. These proved the more explosive during the 1980s, and absorbed more attention than the economic dynamism of the previous decade. The political leverage which the rise in commodity prices had offered to some governments in the years after 1973, disappeared after 1980. The prices of major resources collapsed and traditional market forces reasserted their role. But the newer factors were political. They were 'new' principally in the importance which they gained in international relations and for their place in affecting world stability and order, as opposed to the purely regional relevance which many of these factors had previously enjoyed.

On the face of things neither Marx nor Massachusetts, with its historical commitment to democracy and liberty, had as much relevance as Machiavelli to international politics in the 1980s. He had stressed the need for stable frontiers and secure rule. But even his political and non-ideological understanding of international relations was inhibited by the demands of powerful ideologies.

Race cut across other ideological and political factors in the 1980s as it had done before. There was, however, evidence that racial forces were more active. Mistrust of American and North and West European influence was at least partly racial. The impact of the Arab initiative in raising the price of oil and the simultaneous success of the Vietnamese effectively divided international relations along racial barriers. The push of the latter into the other states of Indochina was linked to the protection of their ethnic identity and the rejection of that of the Chinese. The emigration of the so-called 'boat people' following the fall of Saigon in 1975 was a demonstration that the belief in racial unity was as strong as at any earlier period. The argument that racial community was the basis of political community existed elsewhere, notably in Africa. The presence of the Cubans on the continent, long after their first entry in support of Soviet-backed forces in the war between Somalia and Ethiopia in 1977, was tied to this belief. Although only a minority of the Cuban population was of negro descent, they claimed to represent the freeing of black peoples, a substantial token of the cultural connections between the African negro and the Creole and negro communities in the western hemisphere. The Cubans therefore suggested an ideological presence in Africa, fighting with the Angolans against the insurgents assisted by the white government of South Africa. They were more than mere agents of the Soviet Union. Indeed by 1984 there was a degree of tension between the Soviet and Cuban governments. Fidel Castro did not attend the 1984 meeting of COMECON states in Moscow, protesting against the failure of the Soviet Union to condemn more strongly than it did the invasion of Grenada by the troops of the United States. The stress on racial identity cut across the internationalist class arguments of communism. There was no prospect that economic and social progress could eliminate the natural distinctions of race.

Identity of racial, cultural and political community existed among the Moslems. This was alleged to be a significant factor in the internal political development of the Soviet federation; Moslem populations in the southern republics were growing faster than the other peoples of the union. However outside the Soviet Union and its centralised party organisation, the internationalism of Islam was of a different kind from that of international communism. Moreover it was the religious not the racial element that proved the more dynamic in the 1980s.

The religious ideology of Islam stood aside from the competition between capitalism and communism. The revitalised Islamic culture of the later twentieth century was fundamentally alien to Marxism. It was exclusive, affording no hope for the non-believers who could not become acceptable through the evolution of class and economy. Capitalism and democratic politics were irrelevant to a movement that drew absolute distinctions based on religion. Any concept of compromise in the interests of a balance of power was also fundamentally alien to this ideology.

The rejection of compromise and the need for a balance of power was in effect a rejection of the political in international relations. The Iranian rejection of any terms short of the destruction of a regime was in contrast to those of the United Kingdom in the war with the Argentine. Local surrender ended that war in 1982. Ironically the government which had ordered the original invasion of the Falkland Islands fell as a result of domestic political pressures. The claim that only total victory was acceptable meant no negotiation and many groups with political demands operated on that basis during the 1980s. Groups demanding a change of policy left no room for negotiation. The many Middle Eastern groups requiring an unqualified change of policy, particularly on the part of the government of the USA towards Israel and the Palestinian political future, expected only the capitulation of the state. No established state could be expected to do this. Once the authority of the state had been successfully challenged, the principle of sovereignty in international relations was overthrown.[6] In effect the United States was subjected to a 'war' in the conflict with hostile groups who wished no argument, and offered little if any scope for balanced concession.

Anti-American attacks—bombs placed on military and other premises, the assassination of personnel—allowed no negotiation. These outrages, of which there were several during the 1980s, had little connection with the international politics of Soviet and United States relations. Where these states conducted their relations on the basis of political balance, the international terrorist was essentially outside regular international relations, denying the relevance of the politics of compromise. President Reagan made his belief clear. Much of the random violence in public places was directed at the USA. Many officials and military had been victims in the years 1981–86. American aircraft, tourists and diplomats remained the targets of groups with no political dimension to their policy; that is, they required total success and no discussion of compromise. The fundamentally non-political nature of such activists, especially those working in the Middle East, was recognised by the two superpowers. The government of the Soviet Union was quick to condemn any act of arbitrary terror and any association between a state such as Libya with active groups like the Abu Nidal Palestinians. These suspicions had led to a cooling of relations between Colonel Gadaffi and the Soviet leadership on the occasion of his visit to Moscow in 1985. There were few benefits that came from the visit, and the Libyan government began to improve relations with neighbouring states afterwards. A treaty with Morocco followed the visit, and talks began in preparation for a possible official meeting between the Libyans and the government of Algeria, previously hostile to Libya.

While ideologically motivated movements cut across US–USSR relations, the superpowers attempted to reassert their dominance. The attempts were not always successful. There was no assurance that the Libyan regime could control the support for extreme Palestinian groups which had come to Libya, and neighbouring Tunisia, after the war in 1982. The extension of violence into the territory of several states and against the citizens of many states whose governments were regarded as tepid in their support for the Palestinian cause, shared the essential apolitical quality of Islamic theology. No compromise or 'balance' was contemplated or acceptable. The war was thus a 'holy war', not a conflict based on the principle of mutual and balanced advantage. The Palestinian issue was particularly of this kind.

The Palestinians were a truly Islamic people. Their demand

for recognition and for a state allowed little room for negotiation, except among a few of their people. This demand made on behalf of this sad and divided community, ignored the many disagreements which existed among them. Much of the confusion of Middle Eastern politics in the 1980s came from the internal disputes between different tendencies among Moslems, the more progressive and the more reactionary, and the apparent agreement on the demand for a Palestinian state. Therefore distinct Islamic movements could separate Iraq and Syria and Libya, and could produce vicious fighting like that unleashed in Beirut after the Israeli invasion of 1982. Yet the ideologically coherent demand made on behalf of the Palestinians allowed no political compromise or concession. This was an aspect of 'fundamentalism' in the real sense; there was no questioning a fundamental statement.

The international results of this confusion were most dramatically shown in the evolution of Palestinian 'terrorism', and the reaction which this drew in the 1980s. Growing resistance to the extreme and uncompromising demands left all Islamic communities and the governments little option; they opposed violence against those who supported the Palestinians. The force of this clash between the world of political balance and that of ideological exclusivity was acutely experienced in the hostility between the United States and the government of Colonel Gadaffi and the state of Libya. The President denounced the Libyan regime soon after taking office in 1981. He continued the theme when two Libyan planes were shot down in a dogfight with American planes in an incident in the Gulf of Sirte in August 1981.[7] Whilst the government of Libya claimed sovereignty over the Gulf of Sirte, the United States claimed that the Gulf was international water, and used the overflying of the Gulf to draw Libyan aircraft in defence of the claim to sovereignty. The result was a military success over Libya. The continuing attacks on citizens of the USA and the perpetual support for 'terrorist' violence which seemed to emanate from Libya and their former embassies, now People's Bureaux, provoked a damaging air attack on Libyan cities and defences in April 1986.[8] The need to respond to an ideology which was determinedly fatalistic and absolute, had no connection with the diplomacy between East and West. It was a reply to a view that recognised no legitimate disagreement or opposition.

There had been such ideological forces before the 1980s, but they were largely subordinated to the broader contest between East and West, in which ideology was part of the balance of power. An acceptance of the 'evil adversary' had evolved between USA and USSR. Each acknowledged the right to live according to different principles. The forceful ideologies which came into prominence in the 1980s made no such concession.

The ideologies which permitted no negotiation and no recognition of legitimate disagreement, were also opposed in an important sense to the idea of the state. The state as politics, as an institution for the reconciliation of internal differences and the vehicle for the diplomatic negotiation of international disputes, was not readily accepted. At first sight this was not clear. The aim of many of the more successful and more aggressive movements of the period were nationalist; the respected and established goal was the creation of a new state based on national identity. But there were many strange features. Such movements were also internationalist in spirit. The validity of the nation did not clash with the existence of other nations, but was complementary. The idea was not new; it had been present in the nationalism of nineteenth-century nationalists like Mazzini. Yet in the ideological fervour of the late twentieth century the absolute recognition of the nation to exist went arm in arm with subordination to an international ideal. This nationalism therefore did not recognise the full sovereignty of the state. Such was the political content of much Middle Eastern nationalism. The roots of this idea were embedded in the Turkish Empire, with its system of local sovereigns or Sultans. It had a more recent form in the United Arab Republic of the 1950s. There was therefore a contradiction within the ideology which appealed to both national and international goals.

The Islamic movements of the 1970s and 1980s were clear examples of this ambiguity. The need to build a stable state in places where this was lacking coexisted with an international religious idealism. Islam knew no political frontiers. Arab governments stressed the transnational quality of their belief and were thus committed to the support of their community of faithful believers. However the practical demands of administration upset this harmony, as it had in nineteenth-century Europe. An Arab people, loyal to Islam, were also engaged in state-building. The Palestinians presented the most acute example of the tension between national and international aspirations. Not only were they drawn into fighting among themselves, in particular in Beirut after the Israeli operation in 1982, but the nature of their political need to form a defined nation-state led to clashes with other Islamic peoples and governments. In 1970 the conflict had been with the government of Jordan. In the 1980s it was with the governments of Lebanon and Syria. The Palestinian cause was therefore totally ambiguous. The appeal was across frontiers and nations, to an Islamic idealism. The practical necessity was to determine where to build a state and how that state was to be administered. Harmony had to be replaced by competition and uncertainty.

In addition Islamic nationalism could also be radical, complicating further the loyalty to international Moslem ideals. In Libya, and even in Iraq, a radical political solution was sought which was not acceptable to many of the established Arab states like Jordan or Saudi Arabia, or more especially to the Gulf states which were facing the possibility of declining wealth in the 1980s as oil prices dropped and the war between Iraq and Iran continued. The radicalism of the state of Iran was less relevant in this turmoil of national and international aspirations because the Iranians were not Arab peoples for the most part, and outside the mainstream of Middle Eastern politics. The pressure for the creation of distinct nation states despite the religious international bonds was more important than any division on the basis of communism or democratic capitalism. Any correlation with the conflict between the United States and the Soviet Union was of secondary importance. Nationalism was the more powerful force. Indeed some peoples had fought both Soviet and American-backed regimes in pursuit of their recognition as autonomous nations. This had occurred in Eritrea. The popular movement had fought the Imperial regime which had been supported by the United States as a force standing against

Marxism in that part of Africa. After the fall of the Ethiopian Empire and the establishment of a Marxist government with Soviet aid, there was still no recognition of an independent Eritrea. The popular movement continued the struggle for national identity into the 1980s.

Other cases were less clear-cut. Close association with one of the superpowers obscured the nationalism. Yet no sure path was opened for the USSR or the USA in handling such movements. Nationalism was a fickle partner, often happy to receive both guns and butter from great allies, but providing no assurance for future loyalties. Thus international ideals clashed with the competitive edge of nationalism and state-building. This was all the more so when there was no certainty that the state could be built, as with the Palestinian peoples.

The results of such assertive nationalism did enhance balance and order. The superpowers might be carried along willy-nilly, as was the case with the Soviet Union and support for Vietnam. Defence of Vietnamese communism merged with national, even racial ambitions and finally brought fighting between different communist factions as the Vietnamese armies moved into Kampuchea and against the Khmer Rouge. Moreover, there were few certainties that either superpower could depend on a definite commitment from many of the nationalist movements. National aims submerged other considerations in the struggle for control over a state and administration; later different views could appear in which the earlier allies might be forgotten. The USA had few assurances that support for the anti-government factions and popular movements in Afghanistan would, if ever successful, actually remain wedded to the western political views. Much the same could be said during the 1980s for the vacillating commitment of the United States to the anti-government forces in Angola. The UNITA movement of Joseph Savimbi, drawing on support from Zaire and from the Republic of South Africa, claimed a broadly western loyalty and had benefited from help from the United States. However there was no secure reason for arguing that this would remain the case.

The appeal to nationalism brought further complications which pushed the East–West division into the background. There was often little certainty which among competing groups, actually did represent the nation. Nationalism was open to manipulation and the unchallengeable claims of many to represent the people. The United States faced precisely this difficulty in listening to opposition groups from many countries, including Angola and Afghanistan where there was no guarantee who spoke for the nation; indeed, the nation scarcely existed. When a national movement made no wider appeal to international communism or Islam or western values, but solely to its own people and identity, there were no grounds for superpower intervention. So it was with the demand for an independent Kurdistan. The Kurdish rebellion found little support. It had been sustained in what became Turkey, Iran and Iraq since the first clashes with the government in Ankara in 1925. However the movement threatened an ally of the United States, Turkey, a former radical partner of the Soviet Union, Iraq, and even posed an oblique threat to the frontiers of Syria, as well as to Iran. The political results of assisting the Kurds and weakening Iran and/or Iraq were so incalculable that no outside power could contemplate such a policy. Nationalism and the need to secure the state were paramount, but the appeal to some wider and grander ideal could bring advantage. In this the Palestinians were a dynamic political force and the Kurds a lost and forgotten rebellion.

The drive for the creation of the nation-state and the subordination of states to a wider ideology took more precise form during the 1980s. Independent sovereignty was not enough. Even in the African conflicts a dimension of 'pan-Africanism' implied the subordination of the states to a different ideal, and one which had barely existed in so sharp a focus as in the decade 1975–85.[9] The common identity of 'front-line states', facing the Republic of South Africa and the principles that it embodied, contained the seeds of such an 'international nationalism'. This was closely related to the almost federal bonds between Arab peoples, and like those bonds the presence of a culturally alien state encouraged the supranational ideology. In these circumstances the delineation of an East/West divide, communist and democratic free market, was scarcely relevant. The Soviet Union had direct experience of this irrelevance. The Marxist government of Angola was obliged to compromise with western business, and thus indirectly with governments, in order to realise the assets which the state possessed. The pressure of serious famine in Ethiopia in 1984 and 1985 pulled the Marxist regime closer to western governments and relief organisations. The mass of elementary detail required the compromise. The conditions in which Royal Air Force relief aircraft and units might work became a matter between the British government and that of Ethiopia.

The ideological tension of the 1980s was therefore without clear precedent. The lines were less well-defined between East and West than in earlier years, representing a decline in the easy achievement of order and political accommodation between rival beliefs. The development from Cold War through détente had been a triumph for politics and the reconciliation of conflict. From unqualified hostility which at various moments demanded victory, 'roll-back' of communism or the burying of capitalism, a balance of power had been managed. The relations of the USA and the Soviet Union governed by a kind of counterpoise, were constantly adjusted to take account of changes. Their immense military and economic power and political dominance in international politics, was controlled through the institutions of their dialogue, the alliances, the arms talks, the orthodox channels of diplomacy. But the strident ideologies of the 1970s and 1980s did not temper rivalry with any conception of the balance of power. The racial, religious and nationalist claims were absolute and not negotiable beyond a few marginal points. Precise territorial boundaries and the details of transition were negotiable but not the principles. Total victory and capitulation were demanded. The ideology in Iran required the removal of the President and regime in Iraq once the war had begun in 1980. Nationalism might allow the discussion of how a separate or federal community might emerge, that it would emerge as an autonomous political community was not open to compromise. Many of the European nationalist movements had been content to discuss nationalism within the context of the existing state, but this was less usual, and perhaps less possible outside Europe, where an electoral voice was politically audible from regional groups.

The diplomatic will to seek a balance of power was less

apparent in the international relations of the 1980s. The Soviet Union and the United States still regulated the clash between their ideologies and arms by striving for balance, but the new forces whose presence so strongly characterised the 1980s, were not amenable to political accommodation. These forces lacked the political drive which a stable balance required. The result was a world which was less orderly. Fewer of the presuppositions on which these qualities of international politics were based, remained unchallenged.

International relations were therefore focused on the conditions which might allow a reassertion of superpower status and control. The USA and the Soviet Union functioned in a totally changed international environment. Arms, economic aid and political support were still sought from Washington or Moscow, but these benefits came on terms increasingly controlled by the recipients. Neither East nor West could impose solutions, try as they might, in the way that the French Minister, Michel Jobert had implied when he referred to superpower 'condominium' in 1973. The position was new. Changed circumstances had arisen, if not precisely since 1980 certainly since the late 1970s. The relations between industrial states and the many different categories of less developed states had changed before the decade of the 1980s.[10] Prices dropped and economic growth occurred in states and regions with no settled political balance. This was most notably the case in the Pacific and the manufacturing states of the Far East. No division of political spoils nor choice between capitalism and communism were relevant to these developments. There was a need henceforth for the two superpowers to re-establish their authority and influence in order to retain their status in the last years of the century.

NOTES

1. *Public Papers, President Reagan* Washington 1981, p. 57.
2. F. Halliday, *The Making of the Second Cold War* (Penguin, Harmondsworth, 1982), pp. 56-7, p. 79.
3. Dr David Owen, *loc. cit.,* p. 3.
4. See Chapter 2, p. 63.

5. *Le Monde,* 9 May 1986.
6. This argument is sharply developed by P. Furlong, 'Political terrorism in Italy: responses, reactions and immobilism', in Juliet Lodge, *Terrorism: a Challenge to the State* (Oxford U.P., 1981), p. 87.
7. *Public Papers, President Reagan,* p. 722.
8. The formidable attack was made in response to terrorist bombings which had caused American casualties, including some in a West Berlin nightclub frequented by US servicemen. The argument was directed against the United States on the grounds that the response in April was excessive since civilian casualties were caused. There were precedents in the 1980s, the French raid on Baalbek in 1982 and that of the Israeli airforce on PLO headquarters in Tunis in 1985.
9. J. Day, *International Nationalism* (Routledge & Kegan Paul, New York, 1967).
10. P.F. Drucker, 'The changed world economy', *Foreign Affairs,* Spring 1985, pp. 768-91.

Epilogue

There can be nothing as grand as a conclusion to a work concerned with contemporary events. We all wait to see what will happen next. However since this work has not been a narrative of the years 1980–85 or 1986, there are a number of pointers which stand out from the experience of the first half of a decade. The period after the reappraisal of the foreign policy of the United States and the almost simultaneous rise in the oil price, transformed international relations between 1973 and 1985. If 1980 was not a turningpoint, then the years after 1980 brought an awareness of the great shifts in power and influence.

A sad lack of prominence has been given to the United Nations Organisation during the 1980s. The efforts in welfare and humanitarian undertakings by the many agencies of the UN, and the peace-keeping forces stationed in such places as the frontiers in the Middle East and in Cyprus, made unquestioned contributions to the possibility of stable government and order. These were not new nor peculiar to the decade. The political impact of the UN on the relations between the Soviet Union and the United States was marginal. Their direct relations were immeasurably more important. Despite the assiduous efforts of the Secretary General, Mr Perez de Cuellar, other factors bore more directly on the negotiation of peaceful settlement or prevented any such happy solution to international problems.

Many of the more important developments of the years after 1980 were self-evident. New wars in the Persian Gulf and in the Lebanon focused more attention on this general region, not to mention Soviet engagement in Afghanistan. Central America became less stable as the influence and policies of the United States were threatened and shaken. Other developments were less obvious, but possibly more serious for the future balance of forces in international politics and the future of the political interests of the Soviet Union and the United States. Neither state had a strong and unchallenged political influence in the Far East and the Pacific basin, where new energies and economic success had flourished. This reality forced itself onto all governments. The need to adjust to the new industries and the changes in the techniques of production which were less labour-intensive and of such frequency that existing methods were quickly outdated, threatened all political economies. Distinctions between capital and profit orientation and welfare and socialist economies were irrelevant before this change. The developments threatened to shift economic growth and innovation away from Europe, both East and West, to the Far East.[1] The United States of America kept its position in this competition for production and markets solely because an imaginative and starkly competitive spirit was rewarded. The proposals for the further reduction in taxation by the Reagan administration assisted the realignment of the business enterprise of the United States.

The declining relevance of the competition between the ideology of communism and the commitment to a free market and democratic political economy emerged as a constant theme in the 1980s. This factor had a profound effect on the conduct of foreign policy. In so far as the United States and the Soviet Union concentrated their policies on each other and drew up their defence budgets especially to match each other's military capacity, they risked becoming more and more irrelevant and not more crucial to the peace of the world. Public opinion did not help these governments. The world would not accept a view that presented arms control or limitation and arms negotiations as essentially dangerous. The United States and the Soviet Union were drawn into talks in order to appear responsible. The wave of fear and mistrust of all aspects of nuclear power, whether for military purposes or the production of energy for peaceful uses, did nothing to dispel this assumption. Although most arms agreements in the twentieth century had encouraged the development of new weapons and had cleared the way for governments intent on contravention, and one might claim that they had paved the way for war (remembering the Pacific agreements of the Washington treaties and Anglo-German Stresa agreement before the Second World War), the presupposition remained in the late twentieth century that arms talks actually made war less likely. However the United States and the Soviet Union were locked into a round of talks which weighed on their successive governments like an incubus. Meanwhile the politics of the world of states—ordinary states not those exceptional creations the superpowers—slipped away from the influence of the Soviet Union and the United States.

Naturally the two major states of the world kept an important influence. They were valuable allies and providers of all manner of advantages and goods. But they were more vulnerable to questioning. Their place in international relations was less well defined in 1985 than in 1980 and certainly than in 1973 before the many developments described above. Their influence was less predictable. In many respects they operated more in the manner of 'ordinary' states. Defence of their citizens and the commerce of the nation were preoccupations that the United States and the Soviet Union shared with other governments. Their positions were defended with flexibility and without the ambition of long-term commitments. When American citizens were assassinated and Soviet officials kidnapped, as occurred in Beirut in 1985 and 1986, both states reacted as might Israel, France or another state without specific reference to superpower obligations.

However such trends notwithstanding, the revealing and disturbing contrast during the 1980s was between the concern of the superpowers and their immediate allies and the concerns of most other governments. Agony over the application of anti-ballistic missile defence to superpower strategy, over the manufacture of chemical weapons, and the difficulties in achieving arms reduction, were the principal preoccupations of European defence and superpower manoeuvres. For much of the rest of the world, re-arming was more important. Never before was the contrast as sharp between the responsible aim of arms control by a few and the driving desire to equip forces capable of local defence or attack on the part of many governments. Different values divided the Soviet Union and the United States from the fragile and exposed states of much of the world. While the eyes of Europeans, Americans and Russians were on their mutual security, the capacity for making war was growing vastly elsewhere. Different and acute fears stimulated investment in arms, and the economic benefit which the industries of war brought to some developing states merely reinforced the logic of spending more on defence. The expansion of new industries, particularly in electronic and laser engineering, took place in many of the states which were also investing more of their national product in weapons. The effect of this imbalance and contrast between the 'old' world where arms reduction and control was assumed to bring peace, and the 'newest' world where security could only be bought with arms investment, was full of unforseen and forbidding menace. The superpowers might give an occasional warning. These might be swift and rather 'traditional' in form like the blows delivered upon the state of Libya by the United States, or accidental like the demonstration of the lethal results of nuclear accident which occurred in the Soviet Union in 1986. But the contrast between regular and regulated contact between the Soviet Union and the United States on the one hand and the military strength available to governments which were often insecure and politically weak, on the other, did not suggest a safer world for the later 1980s.

Although the year 1980 was not a turningpoint and no single event in the first half of the 1980s moved the world into a new age, there were new sources of insecurity to be perceived in the period 1980–85. They came from the present form of the constant struggle of governments and peoples to find security in a margin of strength over potential adversaries. The superiority of the superpowers was in danger of dilution as all states sought constant improvement in their defence and security. There was an irony in the application of the technology which President Reagan's strategic defence initiative required. Many of the skills and capabilities might be expected to have more use in support of American interests in the Third World than against the Soviet Union. To leave an avenue unexplored in international politics, has always been to invite someone else to venture down that path.

NOTE

1. West European shares in the manufacture and trade in electronic and related industries had dropped from 26 per cent in 1980 to 21 per cent in 1985 of total world production and trade. That of the USA remained at 47 per cent. *Le Monde* 29 April 1986.

Bibliography

A selected bibliography for a work of contemporary history and political comment can only be very partial. The following titles reflect the prejudices and weaknesses of the author who made the selection. The list includes titles and articles that are particularly relevant to the issues raised in the chapters and are supplemented by additional titles in the notes to each chapter.

Much of the raw material for recent events must be drawn from the work of journalists and from official publications. Among the latter, three stand out for nineteen-eighties: the *Defence White Papers,* published by HMSO and by the Federal Ministry of Defence in Bonn, and the volumes entitled the *Public Papers of the Presidents. Ronald Reagan.* This work has also relied on the indispensable publication of *Keesings Contemporary Archives.* Among the many academic journals and newspapers available, the following have been most extensively used, but the list is by no means intended to be complete.

International Affairs, The World Today, Defence Analysis, The Contemporary Review, The NATO Review, The Military Balance (and other publications from the International Institute for Strategic Studies), *British Journal of International Studies, Panorama, Der Spiegel, The Times.* A special acknowledgement must be made to the daily publication to which the author owes the greatest debt over the longest period, *Le Monde.* Other material came from *The Economist* and *EuropaArchiv.*

BOOKS

S. Ambrose, *Rise to Globalism* (Penguin Books, Harmondsworth, 1985, 4th edn).

R. Aron, *The Imperial Republic* (Weidenfeld & Nicolson, London, 1974).

J. Baylis and G. Segal, *Soviet Strategy* (Croom Helm, New York, 1981).

C. Beaucourt *et al.*, *La Drole de crise, De Kaboul à Genève,* (Fayard, Paris, 1986).

C. Bertram (ed.), *America's Security in the Eighties,* and *Third World War Conflict and International Security* (International Institute for Strategic Studies, London, 1982).

K. Biedenkopf, *Domestic Consensus, Security and the Western Alliance* (Adelphi Paper no. 182, I.I.S.S., London, 1982).

A. Bourgi and P. Weiss. *Liban, la 5me guerre du proche-orient* (Publisud, Paris, 1983).

S. Brown, *The Faces of Power* (Columbia U.P., New York, 1983).

A. Carnesdale *et al.*, *Living with Nuclear Weapons* (Cambridge, Massachusetts, 1983).

N. Chomsky *et al.*, *Superpowers in Collision* (Penguin Books, Harmondsworth, 1982).

R. Debray, *Les Empires contre l'Europe* (Gallimard, Paris, 1985).

G. Flynn, *Public Images of Western Security* (Atlantic Institute for International Affairs, no 54–55, 1985).

T. Franck and F. Weisband, *Foreign Policy by Congress* (O.U.P., 1983).

L. Freedman, *The Evolution of Nuclear Strategy* (Macmillan, London, 1983).

F. Halliday, *The Making of the Second Cold War* (Penguin Books, Harmondsworth, 1982).

S. Kaplan, *Diplomacy of Power, Soviet armed force as a political instrument* (Brookings Institution, Washington, 1981).

C.W. Kegley and P. McGowan, *The Political Economy of Foreign Policy Behaviour* (Sage, London, 1981).

Dr. H. Kissinger, *Years of Upheaval* (Little, Brown, Boston, 1982).

V. Kuznetsov, *Europe: Ten years after Helsinki* (Progress Publishers, Moscow, 1985).

D. Holloway, *The Soviet Union and the Arms Race* (Yale U.P., New Haven, Conn., 1984).

I.M.D. Little, *Economic Development. Theory, policy and international relations* (Basic Books, New York, 1982).

R.D. McKinley and A. Mughan, *Aid and Arms to the Third World* (Pinter, London, 1984).

H. Maull, *Raw Materials, Energy and Western Security* (Macmillan, London, 1984).

W. Mendl, *West Europe and Japan between the superpowers* (Croom Helm, New York, 1984).

P. Milza, *Le Nouveau désordre mondial* (Flammarion, Paris, 1983).

P. Milza, *Ni paix ni guerre* (Flammarion, Paris, 1986).

E. Moreton and G. Segal, *Soviet Strategy towards Western Europe* (Allen & Unwin, London, 1984).

J. Pearce, *Under the Eagle. U.S. intervention in Central America and the Caribbean* (Latin America Bureau, London, 1982).

R.K. Olson, *U.S. Foreign Policy and the New International Economic Order* (Pinter, London, 1981).

H. Schmidt, *A Grand Strategy for the West* (Yale U.P., New Haven, Conn, 1985).

G. Segal, E. Moreton, L. Freedman & J. Baylis, *Nuclear War and Nuclear Peace* (Macmillan, London, 1983).

J. Spanier, *American Foreign Policy since the Second World War* (Praeger, London, 1985).

S.F. Szabo, *The Successor Generation: international perspectives of post-war Europeans* (Butterworth, London, 1983).

S. Talbott, *Deadly Gambits* (Pan Books, London, 1985).

S. Woolcock, *Western Policies on East-West Trade* (Royal Institute for International Affairs, no. 15, London, 1982).

J.H. Wyllie, *European Security in the Nuclear Age* (Blackwell, Oxford, 1986).

ARTICLES

McG. Bundy, G.F. Kennan, R.S. McNamara and G. Smith, 'The President's choice: star wars or arms control', *Foreign Affairs,* pp. 265-78.

A. Dangin, 'Adaptability to new technologies of the USSR and East European countries', *NATO Review,* no. 3, 1985, pp. 13-21.

B. Field, 'Economies and defence resources: the prospect', *NATO Review,* no. 5, 1985, pp. 24-9.

Nicole Guesotto, 'The conference on disarmament in Europe', *NATO Review,* no. 6, 1983, pp. 1-5.

Dr. V. Israelyan, 'The arms race—who is to blame?', *NATO's Sixteen Nations,* December 1984, pp. 18-20.

H. Schulte, 'Aussen— und sicherheitspolitischer Spielraum der WP-Staaten unter Gorbatschow', *Truppenpraxis,* no. 3, 1986, pp. 279-81.

Index